Taxes

------ ✥❧✥❧✥ ------

For Small Businesses

LLC
Sole Proprietorship
Startup Taxes
and Everything In-Between

By Clint Leopold

2nd Edition

The information herein is offered for informational purposes solely, and is universal as so. The presentation of the information is without contract or any type of guarantee assurance.

The trademarks that are used are without any consent, and the publication of the trademark is without permission or backing by the trademark owner. All trademarks and brands within this book are for clarifying purposes only and are the owned by the owners themselves, not affiliated with this document.

The information provided in this book and accompanying material is for informational purposes only. It should not be considered legal or financial advice. You should consult with a professional to determine what may be best for your individual needs.

No guarantees or other promise made as to any results that may be obtained from using our content. No one should make any investment decision without first consulting his or her own financial advisor and conducting his or her own research and due diligence. To the maximum extent permitted by law, we hereby disclaim any and all liability in the event any information, commentary, analysis, opinions, advice and/or recommendations prove to be inaccurate, incomplete or unreliable, or result in any investment or other losses.

Content contained on or made available through the website is not intended to and does not constitute legal advice or investment advice and no attorney-client relationship is formed. Your use of the information on the book or accompanying material is at your own risk.

Contents

Introduction

One of the hardest, most challenging endeavors that one can undertake is opening their own business. Most of the time, business owners are expected to be experts in all aspects of their business, from marketing and management to customer service and human resources management. However, when starting a business, one of the things that many people ignore is taxes, and how to pay them.

What many people do not realize is that this is one of the most important steps to take when starting a business. This is not only because paying taxes is a necessary evil, but also because it can mean that they end up paying the wrong amount at the end of the year, which could cause major problems in the future.

That is one of the reasons this book has been written. As a small business owner, you probably have someone, or have outsourced a firm, who helps you to file your business' annual returns. However, as the buck ultimately rests with you, you still need to provide them with all the information they need to be able to file the said returns.

Within the pages of this book, you will find all the information you need to ensure that you produce the proper records and documents to file the right tax returns. This will help save you hours of sorting through all your receipts and notes looking for the right expenses and costs. However, it is important that you

Introduction

still go through all your options with your tax professional to ensure that you have a concrete plan that is specific to your business' structure and situation.

Chapter 1:

Types of Small Businesses

Before we even begin to discuss what you need to do to ensure that you are filing the proper tax returns, it is important that you know the different structures for small businesses that exist right now. There are many different structures that one can choose when setting up their business, but it is important that you know the difference between all of them, as they will affect your trading status and therefore, the taxes that you pay. Listed below are the most common business structures for small businesses:

1. Sole Proprietorships

Many people wrongly believe that owning a sole proprietorship, or single proprietorship as it's also called, means that you have to work on your own. However, this could not be further from the truth, as there are thousands of sole proprietorships out there that hire people to help with the workload. Being the owner of a sole proprietorship only means that you are the only owner of the company. Managing and controlling of the business is solely in the hands of the individual owner, although a sole proprietor can employ a manager or other person for the said purpose.

These are usually the simplest companies to set up, as they require very little paperwork and can be set up at the drop of a dime. Obtaining a permit from various local authorities and administration is often enough so start a business. The start-up of the sole proprietorship is also very cheap compared to other business' start – up costs. The benefit of a sole proprietorship is also the lack of governmental interference with the business' activities, although, of course, there are general rules and laws which would have to be obeyed by the sole proprietor. This only means that the business should be conducted according to the law.

However, unlike the other company structures on this list, in a sole proprietorship, the owner takes full, personal responsibility for the running of the business. If the proprietor decides to hire a manager in order to acquire help for controlling the business, the manager's activities also become the owner responsibility. This can be a very good idea, especially if the business is very small. This is because as the owner of a sole proprietorship, you will be able to take home all the profits from your business once you have paid the appropriate taxes on them. The relationship between the working effort and the reward are direct and clear, which makes the motivation to work even bigger.

Since all the decisions are made by the owner, this type of business is ideal for realizing the goal of securing the livelihoods of the proprietor's family members. These types of businesses are usually maintained and supported by family members. In the cases of non- involvement of the family, the sense of freedom associated with the ability of sole decision making is very liberating and potentially profitable. That also means that decision - making process may stay secret if the proprietor wants it to be so. The operations which the proprietor decides on can be conducted or terminated in a very simple way. The same goes for reports, and they are often not required since the obligation to hire a secretary doesn't exist.

Sole proprietorships may also get concessions from the government. For example, they could get water supply and electricity at very affordable price.

However, one big downside to sole proprietorships is that under law, you and your company are one and the same thing. This means that should the company make any losses, you will be personally responsible for ensuring that those losses are covered and that any debts that the business incurs are paid off.

It also means that if you are unable to pay any of your business' debts, your business' creditors are legally allowed to seize your personal assets in an attempt to recover their money. This is also true should your business happen to get sued for any reason, should you be unable to pay a settlement, your personal property, including things like your house and your car, can be seized to help settle the lawsuit. Therefore, this is a business structure for those who are willing to take risks and are confident that their product or service will turn a profit at the end of every fiscal year.

The other downside of this type of business is that the owner may not possess all the necessary skills related to various aspects of their business, which can prevent it from growing, always keeping it small. The inability to raise sufficient capital is also something that can make the business growth significantly difficult because they have often put all the money they had into setting up their business. The small number of people may also cause a business to slow down. If a proprietor is ill, for example, there are very few people that can replace them in order to keep the continuity of the business growing. Very long working hours may also become a constant fixture due to the lack of people. Many sole proprietors often work double, and sometimes even triple shifts within a day.

2. Partnerships

If you are planning to open a business with more than one person, then you can choose to start a partnership. There are two basic types of partnerships, limited and general partnerships. Usually, people enter into partnerships in order to avoid limitations on business growth which is characteristic of a sole proprietorship. Since a person wanting to enter a partnership doesn't possess a large amount of capital, same as a sole proprietor, they will partner -up in order to enhance the growth of their business. That means that the desire for expansion of business is the main reason and the primary motive for a formation of partnerships.

The rules for general partnerships are very similar to the rules of sole proprietorships, except in this case all the partners share equal responsibility for the company.

This means that all profits must be shared equally among all partners, however, it also means that they also share equal risk. This means that should the company face a lawsuit, or go into the red, then everyone in the company can lose all of their personal assets. However, it's up to partners' agreement how the profits and losses ought to be distributed and shared, and this agreement is determined on the basis of suggestions which are voiced equally among partners. This may provide some sense of comfort when compared with the concept of a sole proprietorship, because the sole owner cannot distribute risks among people.

Since by default every partner is equal in general partnerships, the partnership is terminated if one of the partners withdraws from the agreement. This doesn't lead to the termination of the business, though, since the withdrawing partner's share can be purchased and shared among the remaining partners. No person can become a partner if the remaining partners don't voice an agreement for that decision to be made. General partners are agents of a business, which means they are liable to make decisions, use the partnership property and obtain management control.

Registration of a partnership is not very complicated and expensive. In some countries there are no consequences for failing to register your partnership, but in others there are. Like with sole proprietorships, it's better to fill out the forms for the purpose of registering the business in order to avoid complications with the law. Of course, the first step for setting up a partnership is an agreement between partners. As in cases of a sole proprietorship, the process of partnership business registration is not very expensive. Maintaining a partnership is not demanding and complicated, as there is usually very little governmental regulation involved.

Unlike a sole proprietorship, a partnership is an ideal arrangement for managing a business in which various skills have to be utilized, since partners can bring their different specific knowledge, skills and contacts to the table. However, this conjures up the possibility of disagreements and disputes to be materialized, which can potentially slow down the business and make certain operations inefficient.

With setting up a partnership, the goal of accumulating larger amounts of capital is much more accessible than in cases of sole proprietorships. This is due to the formation of partners, which means there are several people working together to ensure that the capital pool becomes larger. However, when compared to corporations, partnerships are not as effective when it comes to accumulating capital. The fact that this type of business is not subject to business tax, however, somewhat makes up for the difficulties of profit accumulation when compared to a corporate form of ownership. All the profit and losses count as personal income or debt, meaning the tax the partners have to pay is an income tax, not a business one.

Limited partnerships are a little different. In limited partnerships, one or more of the partners can be limited partners, meaning that they have limited liability. However, every other partner in the company will be a general partner, meaning that they will have unlimited personal liability.

With limited liability partnerships, partners that have limited liability will only be legally liable for the total amount that they contributed to the company. However, most limited liability partners may find themselves at a disadvantage because they are also not allowed to take any part in the routine management of the company. If they do, they could find their limited liability status revoked. Should this happen, all the protections that they enjoyed as limited partners will also be revoked, and they will revert to being general partners. Unlike general partnerships, limited partnership can be taxed as corporations instead as a partnership in certain circumstances. For example, if a partnership has perpetuity and consolidated management, then the limited partnership will be taxed as a corporation.

It is important to note that not all partnerships are run the same, and there are various approaches that can be made when setting them up. For instance, a partnership does not necessarily have to be between two individuals, as you can enter a partnership with another company or even a corporation. The benefit of this is an increase in productivity and a larger accumulation of capital, which makes them more competitive in the market. This is, however, not the only reason. Companies engage in partnerships because they think they can bring something new to the market. The problems that could potentially occur with this arrangement are the emergence of disagreements between partners because they became larger in number.

3. Limited Liability Companies

The limited liability partnership/company or LLC is some sort of a hybrid company; it shares some characteristics with the general partnership, and it shares the others with a sole proprietorship. When you create a limited liability company, you are basically creating a separate organization specifically to run your business. This effectively frees you from any personal liability for the company, and separates your personal finances from the finances of your business. That's why this type of organization is has a term „limited liability "in its name. This means that all profits will belong to the company, and must be shared out equally between all the shareholders.

Shareholders in LLCs do not have to be part of the routine management of the company, as this is handled by a board of directors. This usually refers to the persons who have invested in the partnership but don't engage in management, such as family members of the owners. However, in many LLCs, the members of the board are also shareholders, usually to ensure that they are also liable for any losses that the company incurs. The owners can name a member to take the responsibility for managing the partnership, and they can even appoint an outsider to do the job.

The limited liability partnership start –up is more complicated than setting up a sole proprietorship or a general partnership. Paperwork is required, sometimes called „articles of organization", which is then filed with a state agency. A person starting up this company would have to pay a filing fee, which can range from $100 to $800. The limited company agreement contains the rules for business operation, which may include data referring to percent interest per member, voting power, rules for voting and meetings, rights and responsibilities members need to undertake and data about profit and loss.

Limited liability partnership members do not have the right of transferring their ownership. In the case of retirement or death of a shareholder, the continuity dissolves. When LLC loses one owner, the remaining ones are compelled to fill in the forms for closing of their business. If they wish to continue doing business, they are obliged to open a new and separate company in order to do so.

Limited companies are also similar to corporations in many ways. Despite the fact that they cannot be deemed as individuals under federal law in the same way that corporations are, they can still be subject to some of the same rules that corporations are expected to follow. For instance, they can choose to be run as S-Corporations, which means that they can have a limit of 100 shareholders, and those shareholders must prove that they are US citizens. If the LLC is owned by just one person, then the owner can choose to be treated as a sole proprietor for the purposes of filing their income tax returns. Business income is passed through the business to the owner or owners, on the basis of which they write a report containing data on the share of profits and losses, which is then sent to the IRS. This is also called a pass

– through taxation, which enables the non – owners to avoid double taxation.

Like sole proprietorship and general and limited partnerships, LLC also has a limit on business growth. Although it stands a better chance than sole proprietor when it comes to capital accumulation, there are some things that are inaccessible to LLC, such as issuing shares of stock in order to attract investors.

As a sole proprietor, creating a limited company may actually be a good idea, as it allows you to enjoy some of the perks of having a sole proprietorship, while simultaneously enjoying limited liability. Despite the slightly complicated application process, LLC is considered a simple business when it comes to structure.

4. Corporations

As most people know by now, corporations are considered as separate legal persons under federal law. This is what makes corporations different from a sole proprietorship and a partnership alike. In addition, because they are separate legal persons, the owners and shareholders in the corporation are rarely held financially responsible for any financial or legal claims that may arise against the corporation. That means that the shareholders of the corporation can't lose more than they have invested, and they are not obligated to pay their debts if the corporation as such doesn't have enough money to pay it. However, corporations are traditionally large companies, so why would you want to create a small corporation?

Well, the main advantage of a corporation is that they allow you to expand your business a lot faster than any other companies on this list. This is because they allow you to raise huge amounts of capital by issuing stock. The percentage of stock determines the portion of the corporation which is owned by shareholders. Board of directors is often appointed by the shareholders. The board usually consists of people from outside the corporation who are responsible for managing and governing. It inspects policies made by the corporation, outlines goals, hires executives and approves dividends to shareholders.

The corporation has another advantage over other forms of business organization, and that's the ability to get bank loans relatively easily. Their ability to get loans depends on the corporation's size and strength, but it's important to note that if the corporation is large enough, the bank won't request a guarantee by its owners in order to issue a loan, which is not the case with small businesses.

The fact that they are large contributes to the fact that they are able to attract people with various kinds of skills, and they can usually afford to hire high trained professionals. There is a low risk of shutting down a certain operation segment because of the lack of skilled workers, which can easily happen to a sole proprietor or a partnership.

Another thing that sets a corporation apart from other types of organizations is the continuity. Since a corporation is a separate legal life, it doesn't have to end when an owner retires or dies. In these cases, the ownership can be transferred through stock which is sold to other persons. Some corporation founders, however, impose a restriction on the transferability of the stock, turning the corporation into a privately – held organization that way. This consequently means that only a small number of people is allowed to hold the stock, and aren't allowed to sell it to anyone. The transferability also, however, means that the double taxation is obligatory – it must pay extra taxes because of its status as a separate legal life. That means that the dividends received are paid first at the corporate tax rate and then as an individual tax rate.

The problem that might occur within a corporation is the existence of different goals set by people that have different positions within a corporation. For example, managers, who usually don't own stock, would be more interested in their careers than in profitability of a corporation, while stockholders who often don't work for the company would be more interested in profit and would devote less energy in trying to improve the working conditions of their employees. This kind of a complex human structure doesn't exist in smaller business organizations, making them much easier to manage.

Corporations are ideal organizations for raising capital. This type of a business organization is the most effective for a large amount of capital accumulation. However, the costs of starting a corporation are high and it requires a lot of paperwork. This process requires paying the licensing, filing, accounting and attorney fees, which can cost up to several thousand dollars.

Companies like Facebook and Yahoo were able to grow to their current sizes because they are corporations. However, if you are not sure about how large your company can become, you can always choose to incorporate it at a later date. Now that you know a little bit about the different company structures that you can choose from, we can now delve into the world of taxes. In the next chapter, we shall look at the different types of tax that small companies are expected to pay, and begin to take a look at how you can organize your records so that you are filing the correct returns.

Chapter 2:

Types of Small Business Tax

One of the most boring things you can do is go through all 74,000+ pages of the federal tax code to see which taxes you need to file and when. Therefore, this practice is not very high on anyone's priorities list, especially if they have both business and a home to run. However, if you are running a business, there are certain sections of the federal tax code that you just *have* to be familiar with.

There are quite a few things that will dictate what you have to pay in taxes apart from the type of company that you are running, mainly the income you receive from that business. In general, the more you make, the more you get taxed. However, your expenditure is just as important as your income, and it can actually help to reduce the amount of tax you pay.

So how does the IRS determine how much of your income they can tax? Well, just as with your personal taxes, there is a myriad of forms that you will have to fill in order to file your tax returns. Every form is unique in both name and purpose. Some of them are meant to report deductions, while others are designed to help you take advantage of tax credits that can ultimately place you in a lower tax bracket. So, rather than looking at all those forms like they are the enemy the next time you receive them, you should actually welcome them as a friend that will help you ensure that you only pay what you owe, and not a penny more.

It is important to note that all tax returns (at both the federal and state level) for small businesses in the US need to be handed in by the 15th of March every year. If you would like an extension for whatever reason, the deadline to apply for it is the same. However, it must be noted that the extension only gives you 6 months to get your house in order, meaning that by September 15 all your returns for the previous year have to have been filed with the IRS. Failure to do so could result in heavy fines, and even jail time if you are convicted of tax evasion.

Before you even begin to contemplate how your year has gone, and therefore how much tax you need to pay, you need to first get all your records in order. However, before you can even get *those* in order, you need to remember that unlike your individual tax returns, businesses are required to submit forms for four different taxes, all of which cover different aspects of the business. These taxes are listed below.

1. Income Tax

Before engaging in analysis of an income tax, the first thing you should know is how the income is defined. There are roughly two kinds of profit – business profit, the profit used for business expenses, and net profit that's not injected back into business. The latter type of profit is income, and when this profit is taxed, that taxation is called an income tax. However, income for businesses and income for individuals are defined differently. Generally, income includes any type of enrichment that taxpayer receives, which includes profit gained by businesses, rents, interests, dividends, pensions, annuities, etc. Most tax systems don't consider health care benefits to be income and thus subject to income tax. An income tax is a tax imposed on taxpaying individuals and entities on the basis of income as it's here defined.

Individuals are taxed at different rates than companies. "Individuals" means only human beings. The tax rates among individuals may also vary from country to country. However, many countries share similar tax systems when it comes to income taxation. Residents and nonresidents will also be taxed differently, and residents will generally be taxed on all worldwide income.

Sole proprietorships and independent contractors are subjected to a self- employment tax, which will be discussed in the next chapter.

Partnerships are not directly taxed by federal government or the state, but the individual partners are taxed based on their income. Partnerships are obliged to file an annual report on their income, deductions, gains, and losses, but they are not obligated to pay an income tax. This means that partnerships are not regarded as businesses that need to be subjected to taxation on an entity level, but their members are, because the individuals are directly taxable, as are corporations. The character of an individual partner's share of income is calculated on a partnership level.

As for Limited liability companies, they could be treated either as a partnership, or as a corporation. If they are defined as partnerships, then they aren't directly taxable, however, is they are defined as a corporation, then they will be subject to taxation at the entity level.

Chapter 2: Types of Small Business Tax

Many tax systems regard an income tax imposed on corporations as a corporate tax. This is a direct tax, which is imposed on corporation's income or capital, in most cases on the national level. The corporation is taxed as an entity level, unlike partnerships or sometimes limited liability companies.

In the United States, all companies other than partnerships are expected to file income tax returns annually. There are various ways this can be done. For instance, if you own a business that uses the withholding method of paying taxes, then you should be able to pay your taxes as you earn your income.

You could also choose to pay estimated taxes, which means that you will be able to pay the taxes due when you file a federal income tax return. The estimated taxes are taxes that are not subject to any type of withholding. This type of tax has to be paid by individuals, sole proprietorships, S corporations and partners if they owe more than $1000 when they file their return. However, as estimated income tax returns are just that, estimates, then the amount that you need to pay in taxes will be pegged on your previous year's earnings. For instance, if you paid at least $2,000 in taxes last year, then your taxes for this year will equals 100% of the $2000, or 90% of what you expect to owe in the current tax year. This works well for those who have just opened their businesses, as paying 100% of the previous year's taxes may actually work in their favor. It's important to note that not all states in the US employ the federal tax.

However, if you have been in business for just one year, and therefore do not have a benchmark to use to estimate the amount that you owe, then you could choose to use the estimated tax worksheet that the IRS provides on form 1040 ES. This form is the most common form used to figure estimated tax. This helps you calculate how much you would owe based on your quarterly income, however, it does mean that you are going to have to calculate your estimated tax returns every quarter to calculate how much you need to pay. In order to figure the estimated tax, many factors need to be considered, such as taxable income, gross income, deductions and other factors. It's important that these figures are estimated accurately to avoid penalties.

2. Self-Employment Tax

The IRS describes a self-employed person as "one who carries on a trade or business as a sole proprietor or independent contractor, a member of a partnership that carries on a trade or business, or a person who is otherwise in business for themselves." Self-employment tax is usually paid by sole proprietors, and is used to contribute to their social security and Medicare. A self – employed person is obliged to file an annual tax return and to pay an estimated tax. They are required to pay a self – employment tax as well as an income tax.

This tax is similar to Social Security and Medicare employers pay for their employees, except in this case the employer and the employee are the same person. In order to calculate your earnings as a self- employed person for tax purposes, you would have to subtract your business expenses from your business income. If the amount shows that your expenses are lower than your earnings, then you have a net profit. If, however, the situation is reversed, then you have a net loss. The income tax return has to be filed if a self- employed person's net profit is more than $400. To be able to pay self-employment tax, you have to have a Social security number, which can be obtained by applying with a Form SS-5. The other solution is obtaining the individual taxpayer identification number, which you can also apply for using a Form W- 7.

The self- employed person has to file their estimated taxes quarterly. To be able to figure out estimated tax, a person would have to use Form 1040 ES to do it. The year is divided into for different periods within which payment is expected when it comes to paying estimated taxes. Every period has a set due date, which has to be respected in order to avoid penalty charges.

Some home – based self – employed persons are required to pay a self – employed tax. Workers who are employed at somebody's home are subjected to a self- employed tax. If a person is taking care of the elderly or disabled individuals, then they are classified as caregivers and thus have to pay the self- employed tax.

Many tax payers willingly pay this tax as it ensures that they will have access to some form of retirement and disability benefits, as well as hospital insurance. The tax also goes towards benefits for survivors in case of an untimely death. At the moment, the self-employment tax rate is 15.3%, 12.4% of which goes towards social security. However, this percentage is only paid on the first $106,800 that the person pays the tax makes. What's important to note is that self- employment tax rules apply to people of any age. All that matters is that a person is receiving Social security or Medicare.

3. Employment Taxes

These are usually levied against those that employ individuals, and are used to cover social security and Medicare taxes. They are also used to cover federal income tax withholding, and federal unemployment tax (FUTA). However, the federal unemployment tax is the responsibility of the business and cannot be deducted from the employee's paycheck.

In most cases, the company will pay half of the Medicare and social security tax from its own coffers, while the other is deducted from the employee's paycheck. The employment tax is usually calculated by an accountant, or in some cases by an employer. The person doing the calculating estimates the gross pay for the employees and then based on the employee's gross pay deducts an amount for a federal tax based on a W- 4 form which the employee has filled. The person then deducts an amount for Social Security and Medicare, sometimes called FICA („Federal insurance contributions act"). The amount that needs to be taken from company's own coffers and paid for FICA taxes then needs to be calculated, after which payments to the IRS are made. Additional Medicare tax may be imposed on employees who earn higher wages. Employment taxes may vary depending on the type of the business, its location, size and other factors. These taxes can be paid monthly, quarterly or annually. Only employers pay the employment taxes, except in the cases of self- employment. They can pay it through withholding or by direct payment, or they can choose to combine the two methods. The employment tax is sometimes called payroll tax.

There are voluntary payroll deductions which can be withheld from the employee's paycheck only if the employee gives its permission for the deductions to be withheld. These can be paid with pre- tax dollars or after – tax dollars, depending on the type of the benefit the employee has chosen. The purpose of those is to pay all kinds of benefits for employees. These include various health insurance premiums, life insurance premiums, employee stock purchase plans, retirement plans and certain work – related equipment, such as uniforms. These deductions can also include union dues if the employee had decided to join a union, and it can include meals and other job- related expenses.

The employee tax rate for social security is 6.2%, and the same amount is also the rate for the employer tax. For Medicare, the employee tax is 1.45%, the same as for the employer rate. In the year 2013, an additional Medicare tax, as it's already mention above, was imposed on the persons with higher wages. This means that persons whose income is above $200,000 per yeah, the tax for this would be 0.9%. However, all wages are subject to Medicare tax, and there aren't any exceptions to this rule.

There are a number of states that also require businesses to pay state employment taxes as well. These taxes are usually used by the state to cover workers' compensation insurance, as well as state unemployment insurance, and temporary disability insurance.

4. Excise Tax

The excise tax or just excise, sometimes called a special excise duty, is a tax that is usually charged to certain businesses depending on a variety of factors including:

- The type of business

- The equipment and/or products that the business utilizes

- The payments that the business receives for providing certain services

- The products that the business sells and/or manufactures

Excise taxes usually include environmental, communication, air transportation, and fuel taxes. They are also levied on the first retail sale of heavy trucks, tractors and trailers. This tax has to be distinguished from custom duties, which are solely taxes on importation and don't fall under the category of excise tax. The excise tax is also called an inland tax, which means that goods and activities subject to it have to be materialized within a country, while the custom duties are called border tax, which means they can happen outside a country's borders.

The excise tax is an indirect tax, which means that the taxpayer who produces these goods has to recover the tax by raising the price which is paid by the buyer of the good or goods.

The EU has prompted legislation on excise in the middle 1990's since tax borders between Member states were abolished and new rules had to be brought on. Tobacco, gasoline, and alcohol are now subject to taxation in almost every country worldwide. Tobacco and alcohol are subject to it because, since they are recognized as legal drugs, cause many illnesses, and because they are considered to be addictive. The other reason for imposing the excise duty for the EU has been a tendency to prevent trade distortions and to ensure fair competition between companies. Excise tax for alcohol included the rates and structure, rules for alcohol that's not intended to human consumption and provisions for locally produced alcoholic products in many states. When it comes to tobacco, EU imposes the tax for the same reason – to ensure fair trade opportunities for different businesses.

Gasoline is subject to taxation because it pollutes the environment. The same goes for other types of fuels, like diesel. The taxation of gasoline and other fuels fall under the category of energy when it comes to excise taxations. This category also included electricity and other products that are used for heating and transport

Some countries, like U.S., impose a tax on transactions of illegal drugs, and gambling licenses are subject to excise tax today in many countries. In Canada and the U.S. state of Nevada, prostitution is proposed to be subject to excise tax, on the grounds that an extra funding for police services is required because of its existence.

It is important to note that all businesses need to pay these taxes, though they have to file using specific forms depending on their business structure. If you feel that you are good enough at doing your taxes, you could do them yourself, however, if not, it is always better to get a professional to do them for you.

Chapter 3:

How to Calculate your Tax Deductible Business Expenses

Running a business can be very expensive. You have to ensure that you pay all your employees, pay all your overhead costs, and try to ensure that you turn a profit while doing all of this. However, many of the costs that businesses incur can actually help them when it comes time to file their taxes. This is because they can be turned into deductions, depreciation amounts, and credits by yourself or your CPA.

As a business owner, one of the most important questions you can ask yourself is, should I make certain expenses tax deductible? The answer to this question is more complicated than you may think, as different businesses are run in completely different ways. Therefore, the way that your CPA will report your expenses to the IRS is going to be different from the way your competitor's CPA will report their expenses. In short, the expenses that you can make tax deductible will depend on the type of business that you own and operate.

It is important to note that the IRS has various rules and regulations in place to ensure that business owners do not abuse the fact that they can create tax deductible expenses. For instance, if you took a trip to the Bahamas in the last year, then unless you are an hotelier or restaurateur scouting for new locations to open your next branch or business, then you are not going to be able to claim the costs of the trip as business expenses.

This means that when the time comes to make any tax deductions for your business, you have to fight the urge to include all the purchases you made or expenses you incurred and state that it was for your business. However, just because you should not include all the expenses you incurred in the last year does not mean that you should understate your expenses just so that you do not get into trouble with the IRS.

The majority of the money that you use to start and operate your business can be considered either a business expense or a capital expense. These are two very different things, and we shall cover capital expenses in more detail in the next chapter. For a deduction to be made at any expense, the business owner has to prove that they are both ordinary and necessary expenses. Ordinary expenses are usually the most common and accepted expenses that your business incurs, while necessary expenses are expenses that you incur in order to help your business, and that are deemed appropriate to be deducted from your taxes.

For example, a restaurateur cannot claim the purchase of a new pair of ski boots as a business expense. This is because skiing has nothing to do with running a restaurant and therefore is not a necessary expense, and ski boots are definitely not a common or usual expense for a restaurateur to incur. However, the same cannot be said for a ski instructor, who will definitely need ski boots in order to continue conducting their business.

The criteria that are used to define necessary expenses is quite broad, as the expense does not have to be absolutely necessary, i.e. it does not have to be an expense that the business cannot live without. However, the business owner does have to prove that by incurring the expense, it benefited their business in one way or another. For instance, if you are a CPA, you could claim that the rent that you pay for your office is a necessary expense, as it provides you with a place for you to meet with your clients. However, this is not an entirely necessary expense, as many CPAs work from home, or provide their services from their clients' premises.

Some claims may seem rather trivial, but if it can be shown that they are both ordinary and necessary then they can be tax deductible. For instance, bodybuilders have been known to claim that body oil as a business expense, while some models have been able to claim that the plastic surgery that they have had done counts as a prop for their job.

It is important to remember that the burden of proving whether a business expense is tax deductible rests on you as the business owner. You have to prove that the expenses that you claim were necessary and that they have benefitted your business in a particular way. As you can see from some of the examples above, these can range from the ordinary to the outright absurd. However, for many businesses, there are a couple of things that are standard across the board.

Office expenses

Office expenses are one of the most commonly deducted business expenses since there are so many businesses that have an office. Before you deduct any office expenses, there are certain firm rules that need to be followed. The most important thing, as it's already noted, is that you prove to the IRS that you are in business. It may seem trivial to say that, much less repeat it, but if you look carefully at what it means to have a business that has an office, it does require additional clarifications. That means, first and foremost, that your business must not operate as a hobby. If your office works full time, that means that the IRS will recognize your office as a business. This applies to businesses that function only as offices, for example, if you are a freelance writer or if your apartment serves the purpose of being a store in which you sell certain goods. You have to be registered as a business, no matter if your business has an office, or your business is only an office that serves certain office purposes. This, of course, goes for sole proprietorships, partnerships and LLS's as well as for C corporations. Many people conduct businesses in their homes, and many of those businesses are offices. If you want your office to function as a business, another important thing to do is to turn an entire room or an entire space into an office space. The private and the business space must not mix together, as that would potentially cause problems with deducting your business expenses, that is, you won't be able to do it. Although separating the space you use for business from the space you use for private purposes is not something that IRS will explicitly require, it will make things a lot easier for you to claim that the space in question is only for business purposes.

If you run a business that has an office, one of the things you can claim for can be office supplies. These include things like printer and copy paper, pens, staplers, and printer ink cartridges. For those that are running a transportation business, the cost of gas and maintenance can also be tax deductible, as well as any repairs and upgrades that need to be made to your vehicles.

However, despite the fact that there are no clear definitions for what can be claimed as ordinary and necessary expenses, there are some things that should never be claimed. This is of course, unless you would like to find yourself in front of a tax auditor and facing fines, interest and additional taxes.

For instance, you cannot claim your first office landline as a tax deductible expense. However, you can claim any long distance phone calls you make on that phone as a business expense, and, you can claim the full cost of any subsequent landlines that you purchase.

Travel expenses

As office supplies have to be used for business purposes in order to be deductible, the same goes for travel expenses. Transportation expenses are, as are office expenses, the most common business expenses that people want to deduct, so more attention to them needs to be paid.

A business trip can be considered a business trip if you go away for business. To a business travel to be classified as such, the destination you are heading to must be either an office, bank, some temporary job site, the store where you buy your supplies or the place where you keep inventory. However, what's important to note is that business travel is not just going from one place to another. When you travel from your home to your place of business, that's considered commuting and these expenses are nondeductible. Hauling your tools or supplies from your home to your office or another location is also commuting. For a business trip to be just that, a business person has to travel away from home and stay overnight for business purposes, in a location that's outside the city limits in which their business is registered. They don't even have to stay overnight – they can stay long enough to require a stop in order to rest or sleep. Also, napping in your car isn't something that falls under the category of business travel. So, for example, if you travel to another city or country for business purposes and stay there for one or several nights, these expenses can be deducted as business expenses.

Transportation costs are deductible only if they are necessary for your profession, business or trade. It should be noted that it doesn't matter which type of transportation you use – whether it's a car, taxi, bus, van or any other means of transportation, the means itself doesn't matter. What matters is if the transportation costs can be deductible.

When it comes to mileage that you have traveled, you can use standard mileage rate or you can check what your actual expenses were. Both calculations can be categorized as deductible travel business expenses. However, there are certain rules when it comes to the usage of standard mileage rate. First, you have to be in business for over a year, meaning that you have to use your business transportation device for business purposes only for a year. Second, if you have more than five cars that you use simultaneously, you can't use standard mileage rate. If you are a small business owner, the latter probably shouldn't concern you.

You must, of course, be careful while noting your travel expenses if you want those deducted. This means you have to keep track of your car washing if you use a car, your gas and oil expenses, insurance, parking fees, tolls, repairs and maintenance, registration fees, etc.

Also, travel expenses that occur on your first and last day of your job cannot be deducted.

Business entertainment expenses

We've all heard of people going to a business lunch or a business dinner. Since many people cheat when it comes to these types of events, there is a tendency to think of all entertainment expenses as something that IRS frowns upon. But this is not the case – some entertainment expenses do qualify as business expenses and thus can be deductible. Of course, there are rules to this. First off, we need to define entertainment. Again, this may also seem trivial, but gathering all information is your friend when it comes to deducting taxes. So, the entertainment involves activities that are considered to be fun, such as having a dinner in a restaurant, going to a club, to a movie, the theater, doing sports activities or attending some sporting event. What you already suspect by now, even these activities have to be business related in order to be deductible. For example, if you are on a business trip and you go to a movie that has nothing to do with business, these costs won't be deductible. Also, entertainment business costs can't involve any type of entertainment. For instance, paying for a hotel room or buying your employee lunch is not considered entertainment business expense. For you to prove that the entertainment in question was indeed for business purposes, you will have to prove so. In order to do that, you have to provide information that the dinner you had with clients, for example, was business related only and that you talked about business. That doesn't mean that you can't say anything that's not business related – it simply means that the purpose for going to dinner was business related.

Some events automatically qualify as events that are entertaining, but that are primarily set up for business purposes. For instance, conventions where you meet your clients may fall under that category. To be able to deduct expenses from a convention or something similar you attended, you simply have to save the program. Socializing after a convention is considered an entertainment, but not a business event, because going for a drink after a convention is considered to be a rest from business activities.

Lastly, these costs shouldn't extravagant or lavish. They have to be reasonable. It is not clear what exactly is meant by this. But at least you can conclude what is an unreasonable spending. For instance, if you have only a few things to talk about as business partners and you have a 3- hour lunch, this might be going too far. Extravagant or lavish is anything that too extreme and thus inappropriate for the occasion in question.

Additional expenses

Additional expenses are those that occur during normal business operations. These include advertising, education expenses, giveaway items, clothing, dues, and subscriptions, etc. These can be deductible as long as they are ordinary, necessary and reasonable.

Almost anything related to advertising can be deductible. This covers business cards, brochures, catalogs, billboards, display racks, publications, newspaper advertisements, radio and television advertisements, etc. Items that you give away to customers for the purpose of promoting your business, such as coffee cups, pens, T-shirt and other things can also be deductible. However, if they cost too much, you won't be able to deduct them. If they cost over 4 dollars, the IRS won't treat them as deductible items.

Bad debts that are business- related can also be deductible. This includes lending money, selling inventory on credit and such. You must prove you have suffered economically as a result of this debt.

You can deduct clothing that is essential for a type of business activity. That means that the clothing suitable for deduction has to be worn only for business purposes and must not be suitable for everyday ordinary street wear.

If you pay dues to professional, civic or business organizations, then these are considered business expenses which can be deducted. Note that the IRS doesn't like the word due when it comes in this context because it suspects that this due is paid out of personal impulses. It's advisable to use the word „fee" instead.

Educational expenses can be deductible business expenses, as long as they serve the purpose of improving skills and knowledge necessary to the business. This, however, doesn't apply to educational requirements that are considered to be at a basic level. For example, you can't deduct expenses of going to art school.

Chapter 4:

Capital Expenses and Depreciation

As mentioned in the previous chapter, most businesses will have two different types of expenses, business expenses, and capital expenses. Both business and capital expenses benefit the company, however, they do share significant differences. Whereas business expenses are usually related to the day to day workings of the business, capital expenses are related to the assets that a business owns.

To find out if any of your purchases over the last year should fall under business or capital expenses, there are a couple of questions you need to ask yourself:

- Do you own or lease the equipment in question?

- Will you utilize the equipment for business at least half the time?

- Will the equipment that you purchased contribute to the generation of income for your business?

- Will you begin to use the equipment during this fiscal year?

- Will the equipment have a "usable life" that is longer than a year?

If the answer to all of these questions is yes, then you should treat the purchase as an asset. For instance, if you bought your office a brand new Xerox copy machine, that should be considered an asset because not only do you own it, it will last for longer than a year, and it will help to bring in business. In addition, the copier will definitely be used more than 50% of the time, as offices do have a lot of copying to do, even in this day and age when computers and the internet seem to be phasing out the need for paper.

The IRS is very clear on this particular subject, and states that every business must capitalize their assets, especially if they are meant for long term use, and will help to bring in an income. Capitalization in the traditional sense is the ability to take advantage of a situation in order to benefit from it. However, in tax terms, capitalization is an accounting method that is used to suspend the recognition of a particular expense in order to make incremental payments on it as a long - term asset.

The ability to suspend certain payments until a later date can actually be very beneficial for your business in the long term. For instance, if you are a farmer and you spent $70,000 on tractors and other equipment that you then used to clear your fields and sow your crops, then it would make very little sense to deduct the full amount of the equipment in the same fiscal year. This is because your farm's income will most likely be very low compared to previous years. So rather than deducting the full amount in that year, you can choose to spread the deductions over a longer period of time so that they have a greater impact on your income in the coming years.

Some of the most common capital expenses include expenses for machinery, vehicles, buildings, office furnishings, property improvements and repairs, additional inventory, and copyrights and patents. The depreciated value of all your assets are usually deducted from your gross income for a set number of years.

There are some things that can be claimed as both business and capital expenses, such as your inventory and property repairs. For things such as inventory, the deductible business expenses include all the inventory that was used or consumed by the end of the business year, while the deductible capital expenses include all the inventory that remained at the end of the same year. With property repairs and improvements, business expenses will include things like repairs and improvements that help to maintain, restore or protect the property so that it is in pristine working condition. However, any improvements that are made to improve, extend, or otherwise upgrade the value, size, strength, or capacity of the property will fall under capital expenses.

When you are calculating your capital expenses, you need to keep in mind that there is a capitalization limit. This limit is usually decided by the business owner or partners, and their accountant, and is used to set a minimum cost requirement that any piece of equipment must meet before it can be deemed a capital expense. In most cases, if the equipment in question does not meet the set criteria, it will then be considered a business expense.

How to Determine the Depreciation Value

One of the most important things you can do is determine the depreciation value of your assets, because as stated before, your deductions will ultimately reduce the amount of tax you have to pay to Uncle Sam. For this reason, the IRS takes the depreciation into account when it is trying to figure out how much you can claim when you file our tax returns.

It is common knowledge that almost every purchase you make depreciates as soon as you have paid for it. Even the farmer who spent $70,000 on his farm equipment will make losses on his equipment 5 years from now if he decides to sell, and the IRS takes this into account when you are filing your tax returns. To calculate your assets' depreciated value, you're CPA is going to need a couple of things such as:

- The name of the asset

- A short description of how you use it

- The purchase price of the asset (this includes all additional expenses or fees tied to the purchase, such as sales tax)

- The date the purchase was made

- The estimated amount of time the asset will be useful to the company

- The estimated resale price at the end of the asset's usable lifecycle, otherwise known as its salvage value

The depreciated value will then be equal to the purchase price minus the salvage value.

There are three different ways that the IRS allows small business owners to claim capital expenses. These are:

- Section 179

- Modified Accelerated Cost Recovery System (MACRS)

- Straight Line Depreciation

- Declining Balance Method

Section 179

This is basically the only system that is in place that allows for small businesses to make deductions on the total cost of their capital expenses in the same year that they were purchased. For example, if you purchase a computer for $30,000, the normal depreciation will require you to stretch that cost over 3, maybe even 5 years, but the Section 179 deduction allows you to keep that amount in your current tax year. This means that Section 179 allows small business owners' assets to be exempt from depreciation, which is a very good thing in the long run. Congress signed the PATH (Protecting Americans from Tax Hikes Act) in December 2015, and in the process, set a maximum capital expense deduction limit of $500,000, which allows small business owners to actually make savings in the long run.

Assets that qualify under Section 179 include things like tangible general property, business vehicles, gasoline tanks and pumps, office furniture and equipment including computers, livestock, testing equipment, and even signs.

Modified Accelerated Cost Recovery System (MACRS)

This is only applicable to energy companies, farms, and "non-typical" business types. The system is usually used to determine land depreciation costs, and comes with a host of complex rules and regulations that are outlined in a 119 - page document that you can find on the IRS website.

Chapter 4: Capital Expenses and Depreciation

If you are new to doing taxes, dealing with MACRS is something that you should consider handing over to a tax professional, at least until you understand the intricacies of the system.

Straight Line Depreciation

This is the simplest and most popular method used to calculate depreciation, as it applies deductions uniformly over an assets usable lifecycle. To calculate your depreciation using this method, you must first find the depreciable base value (depreciated value) and divide that value by the number of years that you feel the asset will be useful to find the annual depreciation expense. Once you have figured out your annual depreciation expense, you can then fine-tune the amount claimed in one year to show the duration the asset was useful during that year.

For example, if you buy a computer that costs $30,000. You expect your computer to last for about 4 years, and after that period you will sell it for $5,000. So, this means that depreciable amount of this computer is $25,000, that it, $30,000 minus $5,000 salvage value. You will be using it for 4 years, which means that the computer has 4 years of useful life. If you divide your $25,000 with 4, you will get the amount of $6,250, which will be your depreciation expense. This depreciation expense will remain the same over the course of the useful life of the computer. That means that the amount of $6,250 will be the depreciation expense for all four years.

As you can see, it's pretty simple to calculate. It shouldn't be a problem even for those people who don't use math operations on a daily basis and who don't like math.

The Declining Balance Method

This is the least used method to calculate your depreciation value, and it involves applying the depreciation rate to the non-depreciated balance. Therefore, rather than spreading the cost of the deductions evenly over the life of the asset, the cost of the deductions is flat during the asset's lifetime. One reason this method is not used as much as all the others is because it decreases the income of a business more early in the asset's life. For instance, instead of depreciating 20% of the asset value, you will expense 40%. The main idea behind this is that something that's not used in a straight-line method, and that is the fact that an asset becomes less productive towards the end of its life. That's why when the asset's value decreases, that is, when its value decreases in accounting books, the depreciation expense decreases as well until the asset is written off.

Chapter 5:

Claiming previous years' tax deductions

If you are in business for a while and you haven't deducted your expenses, not all is lost. There are several reasons why this happens to people who run businesses. You might have simply forgotten to take a deduction, and these things can be mended. Taxpayers make these kinds of mistakes quite frequently. There are other reasons why people want to amend a tax return – they have net losses and want to apply them to previous years, they gave incorrect information about their returns, or they want retroactive changes because of the new changes in tax laws that have occurred.

The time limit for tax return

Of course, you won't be able to wait forever to do a tax return. Usually, the IRS applies the three- year period, that is, if three years pass from your original return, you won't be able to claim the return from previous years.

Retroactive tax laws

Sometimes the law might play in your favor even when you don't yet realize you are in need of some benefit. For example, the Congress or the IRS can change laws in a way that the change is more favorable to you than it was when you deducted your expenses. If that's the case, you will be able to file another tax deduction and get e refund for previous years. Sometimes these things happen automatically. For example, the law was changed for assets after 9/11, and it allowed businesses to take an additional 30%. In cases like that, you will get the bonus without asking. If, however, this doesn't suit you, you can always notify the IRS about it and request a change. Although it doesn't seem logical why you would complain if something like this happens, this bonus can actually result in your having to pay more taxes if you sell your assets that are purchased after the law concerning bonuses is made. It's important to be up to date about these things, so you don't suffer economic losses.

Net losses

Many people, especially if they have recently started a business, experience more amounts of losses than gains. Although that may be discouraging, you can benefit from this by reducing your taxable income from other sources; investment income, your spouse's income on other sources. You can even apply some portions of the losses to future years. You can carry the loss for two years prior to the year when the loss occurred. This is advisable, because the IRS gives you a quick refund for this. You can claim previous year's taxes by filling out a Form 1040X, which is a form for amending individual income tax return. You can file a Form 1045, which enables you to get a quick refund. If you file a Form 1040X, you can end up waiting for a year for a refund.

Casualty losses

Casualty losses are those losses which occur when some external forces damage your business assets. Earthquakes, fire, floods, and vandalism all fall into this category. If this happens, you can deduct these losses from prior year's taxes by filing an amended tax return and deducting the loss amount from that year. The IRS will then send you a refund because this calculation will result in a certain difference.

Bad debts

The term „bad debt" stands for a debt that is worthless. That's what the word „bad" means. It sometimes takes years for the debt to become bad. First of all, it's important to recognize which debts can be deducted. If your bad debt falls into the category of deductible debts and you forgot to file a tax return the year your debt became worthless, you have up to seven years to file an amended return on that debt. However, if the debt is only partially worthless, then you have a period of three years to amend it, the three – period limit above mentioned. If your debt has become completely worthless, then the seven year period applies.

Steps to amend your tax return

The IRS form 1040X is all you need. Since it's not difficult at all, you probably won't need any extra help in order to file it. It has three columns – A, B and C. The first column is for the original tax return information, and the new, corrected information has to be in the column C. In the column B you have to write down the differences between the information from the other two columns. The form is then sent by mail, and not by e-mail. If you are amending your tax returns for more than one year, you would have to use several forms and put them in different envelopes, with each form containing information for each year. If you want a refund related to the net loss, an extra form will be needed – the Form 1045. The other option is to use the latter form alone, without the Form 1040X.

The IRS reviewing process

Since the IRS doesn't like paying money back, the claims for returns will be examined with special attention. After that's done, the IRS employee will then conclude if you are entitled to a refund and if you are, it will bring a conclusion regarding the amount which you will receive. Claims can be accepted, denied or audited. The trouble is that if your claim is audited, the IRS is allowed to audit your entire tax return. So that means that the amended tax return actually increases your chances of an audit. But, this should be not something you need to worry about. If everything you did was done according to the law, the IRS employee won't discover anything out of order, even if they select you for an audit.

If your claim is accepted, you should get your refund in about 12 weeks. However, if you have additional debts, you may receive a refund smaller the one you have expected because the IRS might use your refund money to repay the debt for you.

If your claim is denied, the IRS has to give you an explanation why it has decided to do so. If you don't agree with their conclusion, you can appeal a denial.

Chapter 6:

Keeping Accurate Records

The only way you will be able to file accurate tax returns is if you keep an accurate record of your income and your expenses. It doesn't make sense to deduct if the records you keep are incorrect, incomplete and inaccurate. This usually sounds easier than it seems, as there are quite a few records that you will need if you should hope to file accurate returns. Many businesses that encounter problems with the IRS do so because they do not have accurate records, and therefore, cannot calculate their income or expenses accurately.

However, it is important to note that keeping accurate records is not just something that will help you in file accurate tax returns, it is also a legal requirement that the IRS takes very seriously. The consequences of not keeping accurate records may be losing your money and suffering additional costs, which is something you want to avoid. If you are a small business owner, some of the most important things that you need to keep are your receipts and tax records. Not only does the IRS require you to keep them, they will also provide you with a means to track your income, deductions and any credit that is shown on your tax returns. They will help prove that you earned what you claim you earned, and that you bought the things that you claimed you bought.

However, it's not that hard to keep records of your expenses. With clear direction, it shouldn't be something you would have to worry about too much.

Depending on the taxes that you are going to have to pay, you are going to need to keep certain documents and supply these to your CPA when the time comes for you to file your tax returns. Some of the documents that you will need include:

1. General documents

These include your previous year's tax returns, and your Federal Tax Identification Number

2. For Business Income Taxes

You will need to keep quite a few records for these including

- All accounting journals and ledgers; basically all reports that contain records of business transactions that you may have carried out, and all the funds that left or entered your account

- All documents that show your transactions in detail. Journals and ledges tend to provide an overview of your transactions

- All invoices that you received and paid

- All bank deposit slips

- Bank statements

- Your business checkbook, including cancelled checks

- Credit card statements

- All vehicle and mileage logs

3. Business-Related Expenses

You will need to provide a detailed, itemized breakdown of all you expenses if you hope to reduce your taxable income, and hopefully, drop to a lower tax bracket. Ensure that all your receipts have their purchase dates. If it's too hard for you to decide what your categories should be, there is an IRS Schedule C, a form that helps you list your business – related expenses. These are not carved in stone, but the form helps you gain a general orientation when it comes to your categories, which helps you organize your business in a good way. Some of the categories included by an IRS Schedule C are:

- Supplies: general office supplies

- Regular operation costs such as rent, utilities, and subscription based services. You can also include repairs and maintenance in this category

- Taxes and licenses

- Depletion

- Interest

- Bad debts

- Entertainment and travel (meals, car expenses)

- Marketing and advertising costs

- Expert fees and commissions for people such as attorneys, accountants and consultants

- Insurance policies, such as individual and group policies, company vehicle policies, and other policies that cover your assets

- Equipment and assets, ensuring that you include any applicable depreciation schedules. You can divide this by two categories – equipment, machinery and vehicles, and other business – related property.

The employment taxes listed below is also included in the IRS Schedule C form. You can put them all together, or you can separate employment taxes from other business expenses, as it's done here.

As it's already been said, this list is not carved in stone. The Schedule C is here just to give you an idea of how to put all your business – related expenses on paper. It all depends mainly because different businesses will have different categories; some will keep all of these and add more, and some might replace a few categories from this list with other ones. For example, a writer may include agent fees and writing supplies on the list. What's also important is to put a miscellaneous category for those expenses you do not have a category name for.

4. For Employment Taxes

You will need

- Employee forms

- W-9 forms

- I-9 forms

- W-2 forms

- Records of subcontractors and professional services

- 1099: non-employee tax forms

- 1099-misc forms

- Payroll reports

- Monthly or quarterly reports for the total time each employee has worked

- Monthly or quarterly reports for the wages paid to each employee

- The gross monthly payroll

- The total deductions held back from employee wages

- For Self-Employment Taxes

- You will need to provide a calculated percentage of your net income as follows

- Social security tax: 12.9%

- Medicare tax: 2.9%

It is important to note that there are some expenses where you will not necessarily have to keep a receipt. For instance, if you are travelling, you will not have to keep any receipts other than the receipts for your lodgings. In addition, you are not expected to keep receipts for entertainment, transportation or gifts, as long as the following conditions apply:

- The cost of the exemptions is less than $75

- The exemption is transportation and you cannot readily obtain a receipt

Chapter 6: Keeping Accurate Records

Despite these exemptions, you must still keep in mind that should you ever be subject to an audit, all your expenses will be called into question, including the expenses under $75. For the IRS to uphold any deductions for expenses under $75 during an audit, you are going to have to provide them with the following information:

- The amount of the expense

- The date the expense was incurred

- The location the expense was incurred

- The purpose for the expense

If the expenses are entertainment expenses, then you are going to have to provide the names of the people that were entertained. To make this easier, it is always advisable to write these things on the back of any receipt you receive, in your diary, or even on your calendar. It's important to note that the IRS pays great attention to entertainment business expenses, because it always suspects these could be abused, meaning it suspects that these expenses were made only while entertaining, without the business element attached to it. If you want to avoid being scrutinized and even closely scrutinized if you get selected for an audit, you will have to treat these expenses with more care. That means you will have to keep closer track of these expenses more than for any others. To be able to do this, it helps to categorize them separately. After you have written information on the back of the receipts you received, it's advisable to make your records as clear as possible afterward, when coming to the place you work. You should include the date, the amount spent, place where the expense occurred, the business purpose and the business relationship. The latter will contain names of people which you encountered during the event in question. Rewrite the data from the receipt, a calendar or a diary to keep track of them more easily. Although you will have all this information on the receipt, as it's mentioned, it's well advised to keep track of these expenses more carefully. Still, you don't have to be too diligent about it – the IRS doesn't require you to keep credit card slips, canceled checks or other documents that closely detail the event in question. However, having these five categories listed above in mind will help you have a clear head, but it will also help you to avoid any trouble with the IRS.

In general, it is advised that you keep your records for at least 3 years from the day that the tax return was filed, or from the date the tax return was due, depending on which one was later.

Therefore, if you decided to pay your taxes on February 13, 2016, rather than keep your records until the same date in 2019, you will have to keep them until April 15, 2019. This is because the due date to file your taxes is April 15. This three year period is called the Period of Limitations, and allows taxpayers to amend their tax returns. It also allows the IRS to conduct audits if it feels it needs to. After the three year period, you are not required to keep any of your tax returns, or their supporting documentation.

However, there are a few exceptions to this rule. For instance, if you made a deduction on a bad debt or a worthless security, you will need to keep you records for 7 years. Also, if you do not report any income that you need to report, and it is more than 25% of your gross income, then you need to keep your records for 6 years.

For those businesses that have employees, they will need to keep their records for at least four years, while any records that are related to property should be kept for at least 3 years after the property has been disposed of. If you are hoping to try and get away with tax fraud, it is important to note that there is no Period of Limitations on unpaid taxes and therefore, you could be under the IRS radar forever.

Accounting methods

Accounting methods are something also worth mentioning. They represent a set of rules which determine how and when your expenses and income are reported. It can come across as something tedious and difficult, but it's not necessary for a person to become an accounting expert in order to do their accounting for taxes. Basics are enough, but should be taken seriously for multiple reasons. First of all, you need to keep track of your business activities in order to make sure your business is running smoothly. Second, the IRS has somewhat strict rules when it comes to accounting as well. For example, you have to choose a method which you used when you filed your first tax return, otherwise, you would have to ask the IRS for approval if you want to change your method. To do this, you would have to use the IRS Form 3115 and to pay a fee. Also, some types of businesses have to use strictly required methods. For example, the IRS will require certain businesses to use only the accrual method. Sole proprietorships, for example, are not required to use the accruing method; these are required for bigger businesses only. Sole proprietorships and partnerships frequently use cash method, but they can use accruing method as well. The IRS states that the most important thing is to stick to one accounting method once you decide on it.

There are two main types of accounting methods you can use. These are:

- the cash method – this is the simplest of methods. It's perfect for small businesses and for the simplest accounting procedures. However, if you sell, purchase and keep an inventory, it's advised to use the accrual method. This method includes recording money as it's received and recording expenses as they are paid. The downside of this is perhaps the fact that you can't hold checks or other payments from one tax year to another. In short, you cannot postpone your income, because you have to report everything you receive that year you received the payment.

- the accrual method – this method is somewhat more complicated, as you don't just record your account changes as they happen. Instead of just reporting received money and expenses when they are collected or paid, you report them when they are earned and incurred. If you have a C corporation, you would have to use this method. However, even some partnerships are obliged to use it, although partnerships, like sole proprietorships, generally use cash method. If you have a partnership whose annual gross receipts exceed $5 million, you would be required to use the accrual method.

It's difficult to say which method is better since they both have advantages and disadvantages. Moreover, if you have to use a particular one, it doesn't help to think about pros and cons. However, if you own a type of business that allows you to choose which accounting method you can use, then the cash method is probably the better option. However, accrual method, although complicated, is a much more precise and detailed accounting method, because this method accurately matches your earned income in one period to the expense in that same period.

Computer financial programs

Computer financial programs are designed to help you in keeping track of your finances. There are simple and more complex programs. However, even the simplest of programs is more complicated than handwritten record tracking. So it's better to investigate the nature of these programs in order to decide if you want to invest time in figuring them out, which would be a necessary task if you want to use these programs properly. The Internet is full of information – you can check each of the programs' individual properties just by using Google's search engine, or you can talk to people who have used it or are using it. If you decide you do want to utilize a certain program, be prepared to invest some time in it. These programs may turn out to be very helpful for you in the long run.

The simplest programs are Quicken and MS Money. They function like computerized checkbooks. They already come with categories, which may not be adequate for some businesses, but the program allows you to create your own categories. These programs can create profit and loss statements, income and expense reports, etc. If you are already familiar with these and are in need of more sophisticated programs, QuickBooks Pro and MYOB might be the right programs for you. They deal with more complex tasks, such as tracking inventory, invoicing, double – entry bookkeeping, etc.

Amending your improper tax records

It sometimes happens that you forget to keep track of all the records you are required to keep track of, and that's something that's quite normal. It's also amendable. It's covered by a so - called Cohan rule, named after the Broadway entertainer George Cohan, who was involved in a tax case back in the 1930's. Basically, the rule states that businesses have to spend a certain amount of money to stay in business and thus have to have certain deductible expenses, regardless if they keep the records that prove that. So the IRS may apply this rule, which is used to estimate how much you must have spent, and it will allow you to deduct that amount on the basis of these expenses. You would, however, have to provide some evidence to the IRS. It's important to note that this rule doesn't apply to meals, travel, entertainment, gifts or property. It's not the best deal because you will probably get only half of the deductions you will claim, and maybe even less than that. But it is important to be aware that there is a rule which you can call upon should any problems like this occur.

Chapter 7:

How to avoid problems
with the IRS

As it's already clear by now, taxes are vital when opening up and maintaining a business. Since you are going to be dealing with some kind of a tax agency, it's best that you learn everything you need to know about it to avoid trouble. Tax systems are tricky – they aren't simple or easy, they don't come with a manual, and the instructions often given by tax agencies are written in a stern bureaucratic style that only few understand. Not all the businesses will be opened in the United States, where the IRS is the agency you need to send your tax reports too, but it is very important to know something about it because it will help you grasp other systems as well, at least to some extent. So this chapter will be dedicated to avoiding having problems with the IRS, in hopes that the information will come in handy for the reader when dealing with their business activities.

Audits

Simply said, audits are situations in which the IRS performs a review of a certain business. It's the IRS' s job to examine the individual's information or the information given by businesses and compare it with tax law to make sure everything is done properly. The audits occur if the IRS perceives a problem with your report. There are three ways in which the IRS can do this – by e-mail, in an office and in a field.

Audits handled by e-mail are the simplest and shortest ones. The IRS sends you a short e-mail in which it notices a problem with your report and may request documentation or additional information that it views as necessary. The most common reason the IRS sends e-mails is the unreported income. Since it has information about the income you gain, it has access to information about the unreported or underreported income as well. Office audits are done face to face. The IRS invites a person to an office audit because of a problem that's more complex in nature. Also, if there is more than one problem with your report, the IRS might invite you to your office in that case. The field office is the most difficult one and you are likely to face a more diligent scrutiny. That's because an IRS auditor comes in your office and examine your documents, finances, tax returns and all of your records. These audits are the most common in cases of businesses who earn a lot of money and who have a more complex organizational structure, and thus require more paperwork than businesses that are more simple in terms of organization.

How the IRS selects individuals and businesses for an audit

There are two ways that selection for audit can happen. The first one is benign – sometimes the IRS randomly selects you via computer, so the request for an audit doesn't always indicate that there is a problem. The other way is related to the recognition of a certain problem. Sometimes the IRS finds a problem or problems in their own computers, but in other cases, they may contact you if they get a referral from a government agency. Also, the IRS is well known to receive tips from former business partners, siblings or other private citizens that claim have an important information about the individual or business in question.

In either way, if the IRS doesn't specify its reasons for contacting you, you always have the right to inquire and the right to get an answer from the IRS.

Nowadays, the IRS initiates all contacts with individuals and businesses via e-mail. If you are selected for an audit, your telephone won't ring. This is somewhat reassuring for people who find the IRS intimidating since the e-mail communication allows you to gather your thoughts and respond when you feel comfortable enough to do so, unlike with telephone communication, in which you are required to give an answer immediately.

Factors that are taken into consideration

When the random selection is out of the question, the IRS uses a complex formula which it calls DIF, or the discriminate function score. On the basis of factors that make this formula the IRS then decides who to audit. The exact factors are a closely guarded secret, although certain information about what the IRS takes into account are known.

1. High income

These IRS usually looks closely at businesses that make a lot of money. As said before, these are likely to be scrutinized via a field audit, but this doesn't always have to be the case. What's most important for individuals and businesses to know is that the IRS usually takes these businesses into consideration and that they are most likely to be selected for an audit. However, keep in mind that not all businesses that gain large amounts of profit get to be selected for an audit, it's just that there is a higher risk for them. There are individuals and businesses like that who are never selected for an audit.

2. Loss of money and irregular income

Similarly, the IRS will pay closer attention to those organizations that are reportedly losing a lot of money. The reason for this is simple – the IRS is interested in the correct reporting, and if your business is losing a lot of money but still exists, it might suspect you are earning more money than you are reporting. This doesn't always happen with well - established businesses that suddenly started losing money – most commonly, if the IRS considers your business a hobby, they might review your taxes. Photography, arts, crafts and other activities that typically don't earn profits regularly will probably be under scrutiny. Businesses who earn small amounts of money but on a regular basis are the least likely to be selected for an audit.

3. Place of residence

Some reports say the place where you live has something to do with why the IRS can select you for an audit. Since the IRS doesn't release information on audit rates by state and doesn't reveal the reasons why in some states audits happen more frequently than others, no real information can be given about a potential pattern. Nevertheless, it does help to know where the audits occur more. In 2000, individuals and businesses in Southern California were five times more likely to be selected for audits than, for example, individuals and businesses in Georgia. States with highest audit rate are also Nevada, Alaska, and Colorado. However, businesses and individuals that were not audited frequently were the ones living in

Illinois, Indiana, Maryland, Massachusetts, Michigan, Ohio, West Virginia, Pennsylvania, and Iowa.

4. Type of business

The type of business you run is also a factor that the IRS takes into consideration. For example, sole proprietors are more likely to be selected for an audit than partnerships, as well as large corporations. Partnerships and small C corporations are the least likely candidates for an audit selection. The IRS doesn't always target private businesses since those are not the only ones who have to pay taxes. Reportedly, the IRS is likely to consider lawyers, dentists, doctors and salespeople for an audit selection. Also, the IRS likes to target people which use any kind of tax shelter or who have offshore bank accounts. Also, any kinds of extra payments are carefully monitored by the IRS. If you have a client that paid extra for your services, those must be reported to the IRS via For 1099. The IRS is extra keen on scrutinizing these kinds of activities, and if they note any discrepancies, the business owner is extremely likely to be selected for an audit.

Conclusion of an audit

If, however, you get to be selected for an audit, it doesn't automatically mean a prison sentence. There are three ways in which an audit can be concluded in. When you submit all information and documentation that's requested, the IRS may recognize that there wasn't any problem that needed to be solved. In other cases, when the problem is detected and the IRS proposes changes, you may agree and comply in order to realize those changes. The third way which an audit can be concluded in is if you disagree with the changes proposed by the IRS. In cases in which you agree with the changes that the IRS proposes, then you will have to sign a document which will allow the IRS to further examine the audit findings. For owing money, separate documents need to be filed, which are available on the Internet. When you disagree with the audit findings, you have the right to a consultation with an IRS manager, and you can also file an appeal.

How to avoid problems

There are several things that you can do to make sure you don't have troubles with the IRS. Since being selected for an audit is a means of which you can come under the IRS's radar as a potential problem, the solutions that are about to be selected can also be regarded as advice on how to avoid being selected for an audit.

1. Be professional and don't file early

If you don't want to be suspected by the IRS, your e-mail by which you would have to submit your report has to look professional. There are numerous instructions on the Internet that show how to write a professional e-mail, so it's well advised to look over them. Don't speculate on numbers, as this will look suspicious. Instead, be thorough and exact in order to avoid problems. Don't hesitate to ask for help if you feel you are unable to achieve this alone, because the extra effort will pay off in terms of IRS leaving you alone. If you do your own taxes, there are computer programs that will help you do just that. You will come across as more professional if you don't list general expenses and give out vague categories. Being specific is what the IRS wants, because that looks more honest. If you think that the IRS will ask for an explanation for certain items on your report, beat them to it; the more questions the IRS feels it has to ask, the more likely it is it will consider you to be selected for an audit. The other important thing has to do with tax deductions – check what is deductible and what's not. If you try to report an item that's not deductible, the IRS will suspect you. Also, large amounts of deductions will potentially increase your chances to be audited. What's large and what's is not easy do determine, since it all depends on the nature and the size of your business, but it shouldn't be that hard to find out the statistics and compare it with your own numbers. Again, if help is needed in this area, don't hesitate to seek it, because avoiding an audit is worth it.

Also, don't file your taxes early. This will give the IRS more time to consider you as a candidate for an audit. If you file early, the IRS might think you are trying to evade something and that you are not paying too much attention to your report, which will make you suspicious.

2. Report everything

That's obviously the most important thing. Trying to evade something will not go well with the IRS, and even a successful income tax evasion only lasts so long. The IRS will figure things out eventually, and when it does, that information will only get you into trouble. As it's already been said, sole proprietors are more likely to be spotted by the IRS and to be viewed as more suspicious. In fact, the IRS is convinced that sole proprietors don't report all of their income, so it's important to prove it wrong.

3. Partner up

This is a tricky advice since it might look like being a sole proprietorship is a bad thing when it comes to the IRS. Although it considers sole proprietors high risk when it comes to tax evasion, this isn't always the case. If you follow the above - noted instructions, if you are thorough, honest, if you don't rush with filing a report and if you offer an explanation when you think it's needed you won't become an IRS target immediately, just because you are a sole proprietor. This advice is for people who are already considering partnering up because the fact that IRS is less suspicious of partnerships will only serve as an additional reason to partner up. Moreover, when it comes to the U.S., in some states partnerships and LLC's are obliged to pay additional taxes. So this advice has to be examined with a great care before it's taken.

However, certain things have to be taken into consideration, just to have all your information – in 2006, 3,78% of sole proprietors that were earning less than $250,000 were audited. There is no rule that says you have to be a sole proprietor forever, and taxes are not a mundaine reason why people change the type of business they are running. So if you think that this is a sufficient enough reason to stop being a sole proprietor, form a partnership with someone. After all, only 0,40 % of partherships were selected for an audit the same year 3,78 % of sole proprietors were selected, so it's good to keep this information in mind too before making any decisions.

Conclusion

Taxes are a hassle for everyone, despite the fact that most of the federal and state services that we enjoy are funded by them, including education, healthcare, infrastructure development and social security initiatives. However, despite the hassle of paying your taxes, the good use that the money is put to makes it worthwhile in the end. Besides, there is no point in fighting it – taxes are here to stay, and turning them into your advantage is something that should be in everyone's interest.

Filing the proper tax returns is one of the most important things you can do as a business owner. However, one of the only ways you will be able to do this is if you can keep accurate records all year round. Keeping accurate records also makes good business sense, as you will be able to keep track on your business' successes and failures, and be able to see the impact of your expenditure, or lack thereof, on your future income.

Regardless of whether this is your first business, or you have been in business for years, as a small business owner, you need to protect your business so that you can see it grow. One of the best ways to do this is to ensure that you have properly prepared your taxes.

OneNote User Guide

The Definitive Guide to Learn the Essentials of OneNote in No Time

2nd Edition

Contents

Introduction

The dawn of the information age spelt doom for the traditional notebook. With hundreds of programs and applications on the market today that will assist people to take down all the information they need, it is no wonder that people have stopped carrying notepads to lectures, seminars and meetings. Everyone from the large corporate conglomerate to the 1st grade student in elementary school is using some form of software to capture all the information they need, and of all the programs that there are on the market, Microsoft's OneNote is one of the best at capturing, manipulating and storing your information.

OneNote has been on the market for over a decade now, and it has been part of the Microsoft Office suite for some time as well. However, it is a program that is discussed only by people who have experienced it, and its popularity outside the circles of those who use it requires improvement. This is surprising considering just how much you can do with the program.

OneNote is more than just a note taker, it is also a planner that is able to capture text, images, video, and audio notes, and retrieve them at the touch of a button. Its compatibility with many of the devices that are on the market today is impressive and means that you can work with it virtually anywhere.

Introduction

This manual will serve to introduce you to the world of OneNote, and will give you a preview of some of the things that are possible with this powerful program.

Chapter 1:

OneNote Overview

O neNote is one of the most powerful note-taking software on the market today. The program allows users some of the advantages of a word processor, such as the ability to enter text, create tables, and insert pictures. However, unlike most word processors, OneNote users can also add audio and video data to their notes, allowing them to complement their written word with audio/visual data.

OneNote is designed to look like a digital notebook, and in that respect, the designers really got it right. In keeping with the notebook theme, Microsoft OneNote allows users to use virtually ANY part of the page to insert their information, and they can do this by just clicking on an area on the page. Do you want to write outside the margin? You can do that. Do you want to move to the top of the page and write something else? You can do that too. Do you want to just use it like a standard word processor? No one is going to stop you.

The data entry methods for this program are seemingly endless, and that is something that you want from any note taking software in the world we live in, where you never know what format the data you are receiving is going to be.

However, data entry is not the only place where OneNote is beating the competition. For those people who love being organized, this program will be a dream come true as it is insanely easy to arrange your work. The different pages within the program are organized into colored sections, just the way you would have colored tabs within some notebooks, and all these different pages are accessible with just one click of the mouse. Information in OneNote is written into pages, which can be assigned different colors and organized into sections. This collection of pages and sections makes up a notebook, which can be described as the digital equivalent of a tabbed ring binder.

OneNote was originally meant to work on laptops and desktop PCs, but with the passage of time and the evolution of technology, it can now work on virtually any system. Different features have been added to the program over the years to make it easier to work with on tablets and smartphones. This allows users to access the program in places where laptop computers may not be the ideal piece of equipment to use. It also allows users that have stylus enabled smartphones and tablets to literally write information into the program, making it easier to gather information and take down notes when the need arises.

OneNote is also makes gathering information easier by allowing the user to search through and index images and audio files to gain additional information. For instance, if an image has text information that is embedded within the file, OneNote can search for it and find it and display it as text on the screen. It also searches through audio files phonetically, allowing the user to save time when it comes to searching through an audio file. Perhaps one of its most useful features is enabling a user to play an audio file while they are reading notes taken during the recording. This is a very useful feature for anyone to have, however, it is even more useful to people like students and researchers who may need to use this feature to better make sense of the work that they are doing.

OneNote has one of the best multi-user features that you can find in an application today. With this feature, it is possible for anyone with access to make changes to your work. This may seem to be a feature most people would not like to have, until you think about all the professionals and students that have some form of group project that they need to complete.

With OneNote, these projects can be simplified tenfold as now all the concerned parties can have access to the information as it is being compiled, rather than having to wait for a meeting where the whole group sits down and makes presentations. The editing of the document can be done at all times, whether the user is online or offline. Notebooks can also be edited simultaneously, allowing more than one user to make changes to the notebook at the same time. This allows users to use OneNote as a sort of digital whiteboard, and also allows users to trade ideas in real time, which allows them to produce the highest quality work that they can in a very short amount of time.

However, perhaps OneNote's best feature is its save feature. Many people who are new to one note have searched the application looking for a save button. However, there is none. Instead, OneNote saves your work onto the OneDrive cloud or a network computer automatically, thereby eliminating the need for you to save every five minutes. This feature is brilliant, as it allows you to concentrate fully on your work, rather than have to remember to save your work at every other turn.

Chapter 1: OneNote Overview

Because OneNote is part of the Microsoft Office Suite, it is compatible with all the other Office Suite programs. You can transfer your work to Word, or Excel and continue it there, especially if you are looking to publish the work that you have done. OneNote was never optimized for publishing works and many of its features actually hint at that fact. For instance, OneNote pages can be ridiculously large, unlike most word processing programs that will give you a specific range of page sizes that you can work with.

Another thing is that there is no set layout or structure to a page on OneNote. This is in stark contrast to word processing software, which always contain some layout or arrangement on a page. Also, a user can load images into a notebook without having to worry about the quality of the photo, as quality is never reduced. Many word processing programs will reduce the quality of the images that are imported into it, usually to save on size and CPU power. However, with OneNote, all the images that are loaded into it retain their original quality. This is unique attribute to have amongst most other word processing and note taking programs, and it is sure to begin a trend that others will have to follow.

As much as there is no specific layout or structure that is prevalent in OneNote, it does come with a whole range of templates that you can choose from. These templates are designed primarily for the user to save time, as within them there are different features already preprogrammed into the notebooks such as to-do lists, calendars and planners, and forms that you can customize.

The program comes with a large number of templates already available for you to use in its library. However, there are also various templates available for download online at the OneNote website and on the Microsoft Office website. Built in templates may be modified to fit your needs, on the other hand, to have a truly personalized experience, you could choose to create your own template design from any of your notebook pages. This is a very useful feature, and it shall be covered in greater detail in subsequent chapters.

Before you get started with OneNote, you will need to open a Microsoft account if you do not have one, so that the program can save your work onto the OneDrive cloud. When you first install OneNote, it will offer you a step-by-step guide on how to do this, and it will only take you a couple of minutes to complete. Once it has completed, you will be able to open the program and begin editing.

In the following chapter, you shall be given an introduction to some of OneNote's basic features, and you will be introduced to some of the changes that were made to the program in the latest version.

Chapter 2:

The OneNote Layout

Microsoft OneNote has some of the best, most helpful features of all note taking and planning programs. In this section, you shall be introduced to some of the basic features of OneNote, such as how to create a page and a notebook, so that you may better understand the program and be able to begin using it to its full potential.

OneNote Layout

Before we get started on some of the basic tasks that OneNote can carry out, it is important to understand the layout of the OneNote application. OneNote 2016 is very similar in appearance to its predecessor, but there are a few minor changes that you may have to get used to.

At the top left-hand corner of the screen is the Quick Access Toolbar. This is where all the most used commands are housed, such as save, open file and undo features. Directly below that are the Ribbon tabs, which allow you to explore the different tools that are available for you to use in OneNote. One of the changes made to the Ribbon tabs is the addition of a contextual command tab. This tab allows you to select any section of a table or recording to reveal additional features that can be used to modify the table or recording. The ribbon can be hidden from the display by clicking on the pin icon on the extreme right-hand corner of the ribbon display. Clicking the pin icon again brings the ribbon back into view.

In the top right-hand corner is the help icon, which gives users a basic overview of how to use one note, as well as giving you different tips and tricks to make your work easier. Below this is the online login button that allows you to login to the Microsoft servers. Logging into the Microsoft servers allows you to change the settings for your profile, as well as share your work with others so that they may edit or view your notebooks.

On the left-hand side of the screen is the notebooks list column. This displays a list of the recently opened notebooks, and allows you to switch between them at the click of a button. This column also has a pin icon to hide or reveal the contents of the list. The main page dominates the center of the screen like the other Microsoft Office applications. It is in this page that you will enter your information. Information is entered into pages via note containers. These containers can be resized to fit the page by dragging the edges, or they can be moved by left clicking the gripper on the left of the note. Right clicking on the gripper opens a drop down menu that gives you access to additional features.

Above the page on the left-hand corner are the different tabs that separate different sections of the notebook. As was mentioned earlier, different tabs can be assigned different colors for ease of access.

The right-hand side of the screen is dominated by the notebook page column. This column allows you to switch between the pages of the notebook you are editing. It also contains an add page button at the top of the column that gives you a shortcut to create a new page. Just above the notebook page column is the search bar that allows you to find anything within the notebook, and all the other notebooks that have been saved in your cloud account, and gives you a simple way to navigate between the pages.

Chapter 3:

Pages, Sections, Notes and Quick Notes

Creating new pages, sections and notes on OneNote is a very easy and straightforward procedure. To create a new page, simply click the (+) Add Page button above the notebook page column. Doing this adds a new page to the currently displayed tab. You could also right click on the desired tab to activate a drop down menu that gives you a number of options, and click on New Page.

To create a new section within the current notebook, click the plus sign on the right of the section tab. You could also click on any tab and select the New Section option. As was mentioned earlier creating a note on a page is as simple as left clicking on any section of a page. You will notice that when you do this, OneNote automatically opens a note container. As mentioned earlier, this container can be resized and moved around the page at your convenience. If you would like to write your notes instead of typing them, select the draw tab. This is also helpful if you would like to create a sketch or draw something into the program.

A Quick Note is basically the digital equivalent of a sticky note, and is unique to OneNote 2016. Unlike notes, sections and pages though, Quick Notes can be created even when OneNote is closed, and be added sorted and edited once OneNote is opened again.

To create a new Quick Note within OneNote, first click on View to display the View Ribbon, then select New Quick Note. Quick Notes can be dragged to any part of the screen, and will remain visible until they are closed, allowing you to make any references that you need to while you work. You can also open a Quick Note by pressing Windows Key (⊞) +Alt+N on your keyboard.

Closing a Quick Note does not delete the note as Quick Notes are saved automatically as with regular notes. They are saved in the unfiled notes section of your notebook, and can be accessed by opening your Notebooks list and scrolling to the bottom of the list. To create a Quick Note outside of OneNote, simply press Windows Key+N on your keyboard.

Saving Notebooks in OneNote 2016

Notebooks can be stored on your hard drive or on your OneDrive account. However, it is recommended that you store your projects on your OneDrive account so that you can access your documents anywhere.

If you would like to save on the Cloud in OneNote 2016, you have three options to choose from depending on the type of information you would like to save. Most users will want to save personal information such as assignments, grocery lists, vacation plans and financial information. These can all be stored on the standard Microsoft OneDrive account, and can be accessed only by trusted individuals who have been given the permission to do so.

For those who are using OneNote to manipulate business information there are two options. The first is to use the Microsoft OneDrive for Business platform, which allows businesses to share information on their projects with a small, select, virtual team of people. This makes it easier for companies to organize things like marketing campaigns and product launches.

The second option is to use Microsoft SharePoint Online. This would only be useful for organizations that have teams with existing SharePoint accounts. However, it is a valuable feature for those organizations that have a formal team of professionals that are tasked with duties such as creating schedules or brainstorming ideas.

Organizing your Notebooks

Despite the fact that OneNote is a note taking software, unlike traditional notebooks, OneNote lets you rearrange the sections and pages you have created into an orderly, organized notebook.

Rearranging sections, pages and notebooks is one of the easiest things to do. To rearrange specific sections, pages or notebooks within OneNote, all you have to do is drag whatever it is that you would like to move to its new location on the section bar, page list, or notebook list.

OneNote also allows you to move pages from one section to another, therefore allowing you to fine tune your sections to make sure they make perfect sense. To move a page from one section to another, drag the page tab until the pointer is hovering above the section that you would like to transfer the page to. If you hold the pointer there for a couple of seconds, the section tab will open, allowing you to drag the page to its new location.

Moving a section from one notebook to another follows the same principle. This time however, you are going to drag the section tab to the notebook list column and let it hover above the list until the list opens. Now, drag the section to the desired notebook and let it go to complete the transfer.

To delete a particular section or page of a notebook, simply right click on the desired section or page and click delete. Should you ever need to recover a section or page that was deleted from a notebook, you can find all your deleted pages and sections in the Notebook Recycle Bin, which can be found in the History tab.

Chapter 4:

Tagging and Searching Notes

A notebook in OneNote can have hundreds, if not thousands of notes. Some of these notes will be extremely important, while others may be insignificant and not really carry any importance to the overall work. Different notes may also be about totally different things. For instance, if you have a notebook that deals with groceries, and you have organized it in such a way that every room in the house has its own section, then that means that the notes that are in the kitchen section are going to be completely different from the section on the bathroom. To differentiate and prioritize the notes in each section, you could tag them. There is no limit to what you can tag in a note and it can be anything from a single line of text to a whole paragraph.

To tag the text in a note, first select the text that you would like to tag. Under the Home tab, the tag button is on the right of the screen. Click on the icon for the tag that you would like to apply to the highlighted text to tag it. For instance, if you have text that asks a very significant question that you will need to remember to answer at a later date, you could click on the purple Question icon. If you cannot find the tag that you are looking for, scroll down through the tags gallery using the arrows that appear there.

Please note that the first 9 tags in OneNote have shortcuts going from CTRL+1 to CTRL+9. This is because these are some of the most frequently used tags. Therefore, rather than having to access the tags menu every single time you want to use one of those tags, for instance the To Do tag, you can just use the keyboard shortcut (in this case CTRL+1) to tag the highlighted text.

To remove a tag that you have no more use for, click on the home tab and go to the tags gallery once again. Click on the down arrow that appears at the bottom of the box. A drop down menu should open that gives you various options, one of which will be remove tag.

An alternative way to remove a tag would be to highlight the tagged information, right-click it, and select remove tag from the drop-down menu. To remove multiple tags, first select all the text that has tags that you do not need anymore and press CTRL+0 (Zero) on your keyboard.

Searching Notes

One of the best features in OneNote is the search feature. It is extremely convenient because it allows you to search all the available notebooks in your archives, not just the one that you are editing. This means that you can start using the program immediately, and not have to worry about where you placed different notes, as OneNote will find them for you instantly.

To search for text within your notes, enter the search keywords in the search box in the right had corner of the screen. Your search results will be displayed in a window that opens below the search bar. Selecting a result will take you to the page which contains the note that has your keywords. You will notice that on the page, all the text that contains your keywords had been highlighted.

You can also search for text that is embedded within pictures, as well as note text. To search for text within images, you need to activate the Text recognition in pictures option. This can be found if you click on File > Options > Advanced. Underneath Text recognition in pictures there shall be a checkbox labeled "Disable Text Recognition in Pictures". Select or clear the checkbox according to your needs.

If you are searching for tagged notes, rather than searching for particular keywords within the note, you can search for the tags themselves. To do this, select the Home tab, and under the Tags group, select Find Tags. A pane will open on the right side of the window labeled Tags Summary. This window will display all the tagged notes in the notebook, allowing you to easily select the note that you need.

OneNote also has the ability to search audio and Video recordings for words as well. However, like with the text recognition in pictures, this feature has to be turned on. To do so, select File > Options > Audio & Video. Depending on what you wish to do, check or clear the "Enable searching audio and video recordings for words" checkbox.

Saving to Other Formats

Like many of Microsoft's products, One Note allows you to save your documents and notes in a different format. This is especially useful if you have a notebook that you would like to share with someone who does not have One Note, or with someone who has an older version of the program. If you would like to save your work in another format, click on File > Save As, then follow the steps that appear. Finally, select the format of the file that is to be saved, for instance, Word 97-2003 document (.doc), and save the document in the selected location.

You can save notebooks as word documents, PDF files, XPS files, or HTML web pages that you can then post online.

These are just some of the basic features, however, OneNote can do a whole lot more than just create notes and search for data within those notes. It is some of these functions that we shall be looking at in the next chapter.

Chapter 5:

Advanced Features

Oneote has some impressive features for those who have gotten a handle of the basics and are ready to really start using the program to its full potential. In this chapter, we shall be looking at some of those features, and how they can help you to improve the quality of your work.

Creating a Section Group by Merging Multiple Sections

While you can group different pages into a section, sometimes it would be beneficial to have sections that are related to each other falling under the same group. This is very helpful, especially when you have a notebook that is so large that the sections tab will no longer display all of the sections in the book on the screen. Should you want to ensure that you can navigate easily and efficiently regardless of the size of your notebook, then this is a brilliant task to learn how to use.

To group the different sections together first open a Notebook that has a minimum of two sections. Once the notebook has opened, right click on any one of the section tabs, and in the drop down menu, select New Section Group. Enter the name of the group and press enter to save it. The group tab should open next to the + sign on the right of all the other section tabs.

Now that you have the group open, adding sections to the group is as simple as a dragging the tab of an existing section to the section group tab to transfer it to that section group. If your section group has multiple levels, you will need to press the green arrow on the right side of the notebook to go back up one level.

Creating a Subpages

Subpages are usually created to help group pages that are closely related to each other. Visually, the only difference between a page and a subpage is that in a subpage, the page's tab is indented, whereas with proper pages, this indentation does not exist. Creating a Subpage is as easy as creating a standard page, however, to create a Subpage there need to be at least two pages open within the book. One page will act as your main page, while the other one will act as your subpage.

To create the Subpage, drag the page that is on the right side of the page tab across the page to the right edge of the screen, until the title becomes indented. Should you want to make the Subpage a main page again, all you have to do is drag the page to the right to make it whole again. However, you could also move the page to the left to indent it even further.

You can hide the contents of a subpage, and indeed the subpage itself, by collapsing one of the main pages. This hides all the levels of subpages that are present under the main page. However, they can also be hidden by clicking on the chevron on the right side of the page tab. This Chevron means that the page has sub pages, and when the chevron is clicked on, lines showing the different subpages that the page contains appear under the page tab.

If you would like to move a page that has subpages under it, just move it like it were a normal page and the subpages will move with it, as long as they are collapsed. However, if you would like to move a subpage alone, you will have to convert it back into a page by dragging it left, and then move the page to its new location.

Obtaining Text from Pictures and Printouts

By far one of the best features on OneNote, the ability to obtain texts from pictures and printouts is extremely useful. The new update of OneNote now supports OCR (Optical Character Recognition), meaning that as long as it can make out the text in a picture or printout, it can read it and copy it into your notes. Once copied, the text can then be edited, which is a wonderful thing for students and people who work in the corporate world who are always getting printouts to read. It is also a great way to get information off flyers and business cards.

It is important to remember that the quality of the picture will determine the accuracy of the OCR tool. If the image is of low quality, or too grainy, it may be interpreted the wrong way by the program. For this reason, it is always advised that you look through the text once it has been grabbed from the image to make sure that it was translated accurately.

To obtain text from an image that you have added into OneNote already, first right click on the picture. Next choose the Copy Text from Picture option, and position the cursor in the area you would like the text to be pasted to.

Chapter 5: Advanced Features

If you would like to obtain text from a print out with more than one page, you first have to right click on the image of the print out and select one of the following options:

- Either Copy Text from this Page of the Printout or

- Copy Text from All the Pages of the Printout.

In the first option, the program will grab text form only the page or image that is shown or highlighted. However, with the second option, the program will grab text from all the images or pages that are present. Once you have made your selection, position the cursor in the area you would like to paste the information to and right-click.

Recording Audio and Video

Placing and video in One Note is easier than it first appears, and you can even ensure that you know when the audio was recorded by attaching a time stamp to it. One Note will also make the title of the recording searchable so that you can find it easily in the document.

To record audio or video in One Note, first click on the insert tab then select record audio or record video. An audio and video recording tab should appear on the screen, with a timestamped icon giving the date and time that the recording is being made. You must remember that the icon that pops up with the timestamp will be the same as your default audio and video player icon. For instance, if you are using VLC media player, the icon will be the default VLC player striped cone, if you are using iTunes, it will be the iTunes logo.

If you are recording video into one of your notes, a live feed will display in a pop up window as you make the recording so that you can have a preview of what the video will look like.

While you are recording, you have the ability to pause or stop the recording by clicking on the pause and stop icons that pop up on the screen.

Once you have completed the recording, you can right click on the video or audio icon and select "rename" to rename the file. This will help you customize your note even more, and add a title to the video that is more relevant to the note that you are composing.

Replaying the video once it has been recorded is also very simple. All you have to do is double click on the audio or video icon and use the audio and video playback tab to control how the video plays. During playback, you can choose to rewind or fast forward the track or video by either 1 second or 10 minutes, depending on the length of the audio or video.

Checking Spelling

One Note allows users to add unlimited amounts of text to different notebooks. This is one reason why it is so important to make sure that all the text has been spelt correctly. Just like other Microsoft applications, One Note comes with an autocorrect feature that fixes common errors in your typing as you type. However, if you would like run a full spell check in the program that is also very possible.

To run a full spell check, first click on the review tab in a particular subpage, and click on the spelling icon. Doing this should open a pane on the right side of the page. Each word identified by the spell checker can be ignored, or changed depending on the suggestions given by the program. Once the spell checking is complete, click OK on the box that pops up and the spelling pane should close.

Chapter 5: Advanced Features

One Note can also correct any math that you input into it if it notices any common errors. To turn on the Math Autocorrect function, all you have to do is click on file, then options, then proofing, and select Autocorrect Options. Click on the Math Autocorrect tab and check the box next to Replace text as you type.

Converting Handwriting to Text

One of the best features in One Note is its ability to convert If you are one of those people that uses a tablet PC or if you have a tablet attached to your computer, you can draw or write straight into One Note. If you do not have a tablet you can still draw or write using your mouse or trackpad.

To input handwriting or a drawing into One Note, first attach the tablet and pen to your computer if you have them. Next, open a new drawing and select the 0.5 mm black pen (or the thickness of your choice). Write down what you would like the program to interpret for you, and using the Lasso Select tool, select the text you have just written. Then, go to the draw tab in the convert group and click the Ink to Text button. Should any errors arise during the conversion, you can correct them by clicking on the Select and Type button at the top of the page. If you have written down a math problem, rather than click on Ink to Text, you can click on Ink to Math instead, and the information you have entered will be converted into a mathematical expression.

Should you decide to use the default Pen Mode, you will be able to create both handwriting and drawings. However, there are other modes you can use if you would like to create either a drawing or a handwriting entry, such as a Create Drawings Only mode, Create Handwriting Only. You could even use the

Use Pen as Pointer mode to use the pen as a pointer during a presentation.

Chapter 6:

OneNote and The Internet

Sharing Notebooks Online

Sharing notebooks on the cloud is a great way to get others involved in the work you are doing. It is also one of the easiest ways to get work done if you are working as a team as each team member will be able to access the work from wherever they are. It also allows the different team members to work on the same thing simultaneously, and track the changes that each person makes in near real time. The notes are updated every few minutes, allowing all the members of the team up to the minute updates of what all the other members are doing.

If you are editing a note as your team members are viewing it online, they will be able to see all the changes you are making as you make the, and should they change anything, you will be able to see the changes that they make.

Depending on where you saved the document, there are different ways you can shareit to the cloud. For instance, if you saved the notebook on the OneNote desktop program you will need to follow this procedure.

First, open the notebook that you would like to share, and in the menu bar click File > Share. When you do this, you will be given two options, Share with People or Share with meeting.

Should you select Share with meeting, you will have to select Share with Meeting again, and choose a meeting. Alternatively, you could start a new Skype for business meeting and share the notebook there.

If you selected Share with People, you will be supplied with a form where you can enter the names and addresses of the people you would like to share the notebook with. Once you have done that, just click share and the document will be on the cloud.

If you are sharing the notebook from OneDrive, OneDrive for Business or SharePoint Online, then the procedure you follow will be slightly different.

You will begin as you did before by opening the notebook that you would like to share and clicking File > Share. You will then select Share with People, and enter the names and/or email addresses of the people that will be receiving the notebook, and click share.

If you have a notebook that is already on the cloud, you do not need to open it. All you need to do is locate the notebook and click on the ellipsis (...) next to the notebook that you would like to share. When the menu opens, select share and enter the names and/or email addresses of the individuals that shall be receiving the notebook.

If you are sharing to SharePoint Online, you must ensure that all your team members have access to the service, as those without access will not be able to view shared content.

It is also important to note that you cannot share part of a notebook, for instance just a section or a page, you must share the WHOLE NOTEBOOK. However, you are able to set a password to some of the sections of the notebook to restrict access to those sections. If you would like to share just one page or a notebook, click on Home > Email Page. This option will allow you to send a snapshot of whatever you are working on in the program.

Once you have shared the notebook and your team has started to work on it, you and your other team members will have the ability to keep track of the changes that were made by different team members. This is made easy by a feature in OneNote that shows the changes that were made in the document by highlighting the text in bold characters, and placing the initials of the person who made those changes next to them. However, if that is not enough you can get an even more comprehensive look of the changes that were made by using the history tab.

The History Tab

The History tab is used to give the author and members of a team an overview of the changes that were made to a particular notebook, and the identity of the person who made those changes. The different buttons on the history tab include:

1. Next Unread – this moves the user on to the next unread section of the notebook. If this button is not accessible then it means that the notebook has been read in its entirety.

2. Mark as Read – This button is used to narrow down unread content. As the name suggests, it marks sections

in the notebook that have been read to show that they have already been analyzed.

3. Recent Edits – This button shows all the modifications that were made to the document over a specific time period

4. Find By Author – This button searches the document for changes made by a specific author.

5. Hide Authors – As the name suggests, when this button is pressed, the authors of the notebook are either hidden or displayed.

6. Page Versions – This button allows the author to browse through older versions of the selected page.

7. Notebook Recycle Bin – This is where all the deleted notes, sections, and pages go. If you ever need to restore a deleted page, section, or note this is where you will find it.

Taking Notes During an Online Meeting

The fact that OneNote is fully integrated with Microsoft Outlook and Skype for Business means that you can easily take notes in any one of these programs and share them with anyone else.

If you are using Microsoft Outlook for the meeting before you start taking notes you have to open the Outlook calendar and select the meeting that you want to take notes on. Next, open the meeting ribbon and open the Meeting Notes Dialogue box. In this dialogue box you will have two options, one is to share your meeting notes with the rest of the people taking part in the meeting, or to take notes for yourself.

If you would like to share your notes with the rest of the meeting then all you have to do is select Share notes with the meeting. If you want to take your own notes choose Take notes on your own.

A Choose Notes to Share with Meeting dialogue box should appear when you select Take notes on your own. When it does, select a section and a page to record the new notes, then select OK. Microsoft OneNote links all the pages that are used during the meeting to the Outlook Appointment. This means that you are always able to access the notes and other details from that meeting as they are all kept in a central location.

If you do find yourself in a meeting where it is not necessary for you to share the notes that you are recording, you could open the Home tab and choose Meeting Details.

Using OneNote Add-Ins

OneNote has a number of additional programs that you can use to help make your experience with the program better. These programs help you do things like format your content, print documents, capture data from whiteboards and even share team notebooks. Listed below are just some of the popular add-ins that are available for OneNote, and a short description of their different functions within the program.

1. **Onetastic**

Onetastic is one of the most versatile of all the add-ins that are available for one note. Apart from allowing users to create custom styles for their notebooks, it also displays content in a calendar. Its best feature has to be the Macro functionality, which unlocks a whole new world of possibilities within OneNote. For instance users can now create features like Find and Replace, Daily Journal View and Author Information Removal. There are currently over 180 different macros available on the Onetastic website, and more are bound to be unveiled as people find more ways to simplify their OneNote experience. The best part about it all is that Onetastic and its Macros are absolutely free

2. **Office Lens**

This is an add-in that is most useful on the mobile and tablet platforms. It allows the camera's on these devices to take all sorts of images, including those of business cards, white boards, and documents, and saves them directly into OneNote. Once the images are saved, they can be loaded into OneNote to have the data in them translated by the OCR.

3. **Clip to OneNote**

This add-in by OneNote Gem Add-Ins is a brilliant third party application for use with web browsers. It is designed to send the active web page in a web browser as a single image to OneNote's Quick Notes section. It supports all the major browsers, including Internet Explorer, Mozilla Firefox, Google Chrome, Opera, and Safari.

Chapter 7:

One Note for Education

O ne Note is one of the most powerful tools that educators, teachers and students have at their disposal. In fact, it is such a versatile tool that Microsoft themselves created an entire website that is dedicated to One Note and Education, as well special tools that teachers and students can use called the One Note Class Notebook and the One Note Staff Notebook.

These tools allow teachers and students alike to stay organized and work together easier to be able to achieve the goals for the curriculum they are studying or teaching. It also allows teachers to work together to make planning and executing the curriculum easier for them.

The sections that One Note offers allows teachers to section their notes so that they know when different activities should take place, for instance, meetings such as staff meetings, department meetings, and PTA meetings, and all the notes that go along with those meetings. One Note's ability to sync with Microsoft Outlook also allows teachers to have finer control of the notes that you create, and allows them to add meetings to their One Note notebooks easily, including the date, time and people who shall be attending the meeting. If the notebook that the teacher is modifying uses a specific template, the information imported from Microsoft Outlook will automatically adopt the same template, meaning that users will not have to worry about modifying information once it has been imported.

Another thing that teachers will find useful is One Notes ability to gather information from different places while keeping the information from the sources. For instance, teachers who are researching on a particular subject may find interesting websites that they can use in class. The information from these websites can be saved as a screenshot that can then be used in their classroom presentations in class. The screenshot, once imported to one note, will have all the information relating to the source that the teacher needs, including the page URL and information on the website that it was taken from.

There are many teachers out there that also use One Note to organize their to-do lists for different tasks, including administrative and classroom tasks and activities. Once the tasks have been completed you can tick them off just like a normal to-do list, and because they are automatically saved on to the cloud, you can modify them from anywhere, and on any device that has access to the internet.

Important notes and activities can be grouped together using the tags summary, allowing teachers to have easy access to important items, questions and to do lists all in one place. Should the information not have been tagged, the One Note search engine is so powerful that it will be able to find the information they are looking for regardless of how the notebook is organized.

Teachers can also create pages for different students, or groups of students, in each of their classes. By doing this, they can then file all the students information, including contact information, disciplinary records and grades in one place. One Note integration with Microsoft Outlook also makes it easier for teachers to import student information into One Note, and allows them to update information quickly and easily when the need arises. Even when the teachers are busy carrying out other duties, they can use One Note to record their thoughts and ideas by creating Quick Notes.

Creating Fun and Interactive Classes using One Note

Teaching these days has become much more demanding thanks to the increased demand for interesting interactive classes. Teachers can no longer enter a classroom and assume that they will be able to teach effectively using only a text book and a few PowerPoint slides. This is one of the reasons why One Note is such a powerful tool for teachers, it allows them to create interesting, interactive classes that every student will enjoy. The best part of the interactive lessons is that they can be created in such a way that the students will be able to complete them by themselves at a later date.

Lessons can be created with custom audio introductions that help to explain the objectives of the lesson and the expected outcomes of the lesson. One Note's ability to create hyperlinks automatically means that you can attach links to articles, audio, video among other links to the lesson, allowing students to access the additional information that they need easily.

Teachers are also able to link assignments to the lesson. For instance, if you have an assignment that you have prepared on One Note already, all you need to do is link the assignment to the lesson note and students will be able to access and complete the assignment. Once they have completed their homework, One Note allows teachers to grade the assignments in the application, and teachers can even add audio commentary to the assignment to further explain where a student went wrong, or to add praise to work that was well done. An added advantage of doing this is that the comments added can be linked to the audio recordings that you create automatically thanks to the timestamp feature.

Creating assignments on One Note becomes even more important for those lessons that involve practical skills such as music, geography and foreign languages. For instance, if you are a music teacher, you can add audio samples to a particular assignment to test your students' ability to recognize certain tunes or progressions. You could also test your students' knowledge of different geographical features using the different drawing tools provided by the application. Foreign language classes can be made even more interactive by having the teacher create pronunciation assignments that the students complete by following different audio files to test their skills. The teacher could then add their comments of how to improve their pronunciation while they are grading the assignment.

Collaborating with Teachers and Students using the One Note Class Notebook App

Teachers need to collaborate with each other and their students, to ensure that their students gain the best education possible. This is especially important when it comes to class projects, creating assignments, and providing feedback concerning a student's performance. The One Note Class Notebook allows teachers to create notebooks that have preset permissions that have been specially designed to be used in the classroom and in learning environments, whether they are in schools or colleges.

To create a class notebook, you first have to enter Microsoft Office 365, and click on the One Note Class Notebook. You will then be able to create a new Notebook, and enter the name of the class that you are teaching.

Once the class notebook opens, you will realize that it has been partitioned into three different "spaces", these are:

- **The collaboration space** – this space allows teachers and students alike to edit the information that is in the note. This is especially useful for group work and class projects.

- **The content library** – this space allows teachers to modify the information in the note, however, it only allows students to view the information and copy the contents if they feel the need to do so. This space is best utilized for giving out tests, assignments and course materials that students may need.

- **Student notebooks** – these are the students own space where they can work without worrying about other students viewing their work. Teachers and instructors will be able to view every student notebook in their class, and edit the information in the notebook to help improve the student's work. However, no other students will be able to access a private student notebook that is not their own.Every student notebook that you create comes with a few default sections. However, you could modify these sections by adding or removing some of the sections that were suggested.

Adding students to a class is easy, and can be done by manually entering the different students in the class, or by importing a group from Azure Active Directory or Office 365. Should the members of the group change after the notebook has been created, you can modify the group in the One Note Class Notebook app by clicking on Add or Remove Students.

Once you are done editing or creating your class notebook, you are provided with a preview to ensure that you have created a notebook that will benefit yourself and your students. The preview has two different views, one that only the teacher will be able to see, and another that is exclusively for the student.

Once the notebook has been created, teachers are supplied with a link that they can send to the students so that they can access their notebooks. This link can also be used to open the notebook directly, so it would be a good idea to save it somewhere if you are a teacher.

The notebook can then be edited so that it provides all the information that students' will use for that semester. The specially designated sections in the Class Notebook allow teachers to collaborate with students and share information on a convenient platform.

Modifying the teachers or students that are allowed to view the notebook is simple, and only requires the teacher to go to the notebook and click the add or remove students/teachers icons and follow the instructions. It is important to remember that despite the fact that an individual has been removed from the notebook, the information that they contributed to the notebook will remain, though they will no longer be able to access the notebook itself.

Once you have added or removed students or teachers from the notebook, you will be directed to a screen that shows all the modifications you have made. All you need to do to ensure that the changes are permanent is to click on the update button at the bottom of the screen. The app will then create a new link to the notebook that you can send to the new student or teacher if you chose to add individuals to the book.

Any students that use Office 365 will be sent a notification immediately a One Note Class Notebook is shared with them. For those who may not use Office 365, they could also access the Class Notebook by clicking on the "shared with me" folder in Microsoft One Drive.

Sharing Class Notebooks with other teachers is just as simple as sharing them with students, and follows the same basic procedure. You must first add teachers to the notebook by clicking on the "Add or Remove Teachers" icon, then following the steps outlined by the program, which are much the same as when you were creating a list of students. A link that you can send to teachers and other instructors will then be generated.

Perhaps the best thing about the One Note Class Notebook is that you can modify all the notebooks you create from one place. All you have to do is click or tap on the Manage Notebooks icon, and a list of all the Class Notebooks you have created will appear. You can then change the specifics of any one of the notebooks displayed without having to worry about opening a new notebook every time that you need to change a minor detail.

For instance, you can change the name of a teacher or student section, add or remove student sections, and even change the permissions of certain spaces in the notebook. For example, if you feel that your students should not be able to change the information in the collaboration space, all you have to do is click on a button and they will no longer be able to do so. Once you have made all the desired changes, you will have to click on save to update the notebook and ensure that all the changes that you have made are permanent.

Class notebooks can be used to give out and grade assignments. All you have to do is go to the content library and create a new assignment. Once the assignment has been created, students will be able to get the assignments from the content library by copying the assignment into their own notebooks. When the homework has been completed, the teacher can then grade the work by opening the student's notebook and giving comments and feedback on the assignment as described earlier.

The teacher only section group is one of the most useful things for teachers, as it allows them to set up lesson plans and assignments in the same notebook without allowing the students to see what they are doing. It also allows teachers to create content that they do not want the students to access until they feel the time is right.

Chapter 8:

One Note for Android

O ne Note may have been designed for use with Windows computers and laptops, but for those who would like to access the program through their mobile devices, Microsoft developed One Note for Android. This application allows users to have most of the features that One Note for Windows has, though it is a lighter, stripped down version of the original. The application was developed mainly due to the extremely small market share that Windows Phones have, and the demand that Android users had for a version of the application that could run on their devices.

For instance, the interface on One Note for Android has been designed specifically for smartphones and tablets, and works just as well as the version created for Windows Phones. The interface if very utilitarian, a fact that becomes especially obvious when you use the app on a tablet.

There are a number of major elements that make up the One Note for Android interface. These include:

1. **The Note Pane** – this pane takes up the whole screen, except for the top strip that houses the various buttons that you will need when using the app

2. **The Up Button** – the up arrow button can be found in the upper left corner of the screen, except when you are on the One Note homepage. If you tap it you will automatically be taken back to the section, note or list that you were looking at before you switched to a new page.

3. **The Command Buttons** – located in the top right corner of the screen, the command buttons are three buttons that work anywhere in One Note except for the home screen. These buttons are usually arranged in the following order:

   - **Recent Notes:** The left-most button of the three, this button gives you access to notes that you have modified or created recently

   - **New Note:** This button is placed in the middle of the three, and allows you to create a new blank note with your cursor in the title field.

   - **Take a picture:** This button is placed on the right of the three buttons, and it allows you to take a photo with your device's camera and add it to your note.

4. **Keyboard** – immediately you tap on any note so that the cursor appears, the keyboard shall pop up from the bottom of your screen just as it does with any other Android app.

Writing Notes on One Note for Android

Just like with all the other mobile versions of One Note, such as the one for iOS, the Android version of One Note gives you access to your notes, and allows you to edit them (though with much fewer features than the desktop version) at the touch of a button.

To create a new note from anywhere on One Note for Android, all you have to do is tap on the middle button in the upper right corner of your screen. If you are in the middle of viewing a note, the new note that you create will be inserted into the section that you are viewing. However, if you are on the home screen, the new note that is created will be stored in the Unfiled Notes section of your Web or Personal notebook.

It is important that you remember that the icon will not appear at the top of the page if the cursor is in a note, therefore, you may have to tap on the back button on your device to ensure that the button actually appears at the top of your screen.

Opening notes on One Note for Android is just as simple, and only needs you to tap the note's name when you are viewing the section that it is stored in. if you would like to open a note from the home screen, you will first have to tap the name of the notebook that the note is in, then tap the name of the section it is in and finally, tap the name of the note.

List elements are hidden in One Note for Android until you need them. Accessing them is very easy, and involves you opening a note so that the buttons on the screen change. Once you are inside the note, you will see four buttons at the top of the screen. The first button is the camera button, and the next three are list element buttons. They are used to create a numbered, bulleted or check boxed list depending on your preferences.

Recording Audio on One Note For Android

Sometimes the inspiration to record audio for one of your notes will hit you while you are on the move. To help you record all those moments, One Note for Android allows you to record audio, and will even translate the audio you record to text that will be displayed in the note that is open at the time of the recording. You can record into One Note easily using the microphone button included in the keyboard of all Android Devices.

To record audio and have it translated to text, you must first open a new note and tap the area where you would usually type. Once the keyboard appears, tap on the microphone button and speak when the Speak Now prompt appears. You will notice that once you start speaking, the Speak Now prompt changes and becomes Tap to Pause.

Once you have paused the recording, you can choose to do one of two things, ether tap the screen again to continue speaking or tap the keyboard icon so that you can switch back to the standard keyboard and stop recording. As One Note will interpret your speech and translates it into text you may have to correct some errors in interpretation when you are done.

Adding Pictures to One Note for Android

These days nearly all android devices have some sort of camera, and One Note can utilize this camera to add pictures to any of the notes that you are editing. You could add pictures to a note in many different ways including:

1. **Using the Take Photo Button**: The take photo button is usually a camera icon with a lightning bolt that sits in the upper-right corner of the interface when

you are not in an actual note. If you tap this icon, you will be able to takephotos for the note that you are viewing. If you tap the button while you are in any notebook, a note called Unfiled Note will be created and stored in your Web or Personal notebook. Your photo will be stored in this note until you file it in a particular notebook.

2. **The Photos Button:** The icon for the photos button is usually in the top left corner of your screen when your cursor is in a note. Tap this button to bring up a pop up window that you can use to add photos from your gallery or to take a new photo that will be stored in the note.

Capturing images and storing them in your notes is extremely easy, especially if you are already well versed with the functions of your phone's camera. You must remember that One Note does not have its own camera, and that it only borrows your device's camera to take photos. The functions of your device's camera will be dictated by the version of Android that you are using. However, there are some camera functions that may not be supported by One Note, so you have to make sure that the functions that your camera is capable of are supported by the app before you use them. At the time of writing, One Note for Android still did not support capturing and adding video to the notes that you create on the app.

If you would like to take a new photograph to add in a note page, you can use the following procedure:

1. If you are not already in the note pane, tap it to edit it then tap the camera icon in the upper left corner of the screen. The insert menu will pop up and give you a

variety of options that you can use to add images from your gallery or take a photograph

2. Tap capture a photo and use Android's default camera to capture an image. If you do not want to take a photo after all you can always tap the X that appears on the bottom right hand corner of the screen. The bottom left hand corner will usually have a button that allows you to change the settings of your camera

3. Take a photo as you would usually do, the X will remain at the bottom of the screen, but the camera options button will be replaced by a check mark symbol.

4. Tap the X if you do not like the picture you have taken and keep taking photos until you are satisfied, then hit the check box on the bottom left of the screen. Your note will reappear with the chosen photo attached.

Adding a phot that you have already taken is just as simple, and can be done in the following ways:

1. If you are not already there, tap the note pane to edit it and tap the camera icon at the top of the screen. When the insert menu appears, add a picture from your gallery

2. Tap the add image from gallery icon, and add an image from your selected gallery, be it OneDrive or your phone's gallery. You will then be asked whether you always want to use this source or if you are using it just once, make the appropriate selection and select the photo that you would like to attach to the note. If you tapped always but would like to change the setting later

on, the easiest way to do so would be to tap the Clear Data button in the One Note app in Android settings.

Managing Notebooks and Notes on One Note for Android

Despite the fact that it is a more toned down version of its desktop counterpart, you can still manage the different notebooks and notes that you create in One Note on your Android device. For instance, if you would like to delete a note, you can do so by tapping the Delete Page button in the Options Pane while you are viewing the note. However, if you would like to rename, delete or move whole sections or notebooks, you will have to access the OneDrive app or the web app version of One Note.

Settings on One Note for Android

Despite the fact that you have very few settings that you can change in One Note for Android, there are certain settings that you can change that you may find useful. Finding the Options pane on One Note is easy, as the three vertical dots that can be found in the bottom right corner of the screen are more or less universal across most Android apps. However, the buttons do change slightly depending on where you are in the app, and the menu is designed to be context sensitive, meaning that it changes depending on where you are in the app.

For instance, if you are on the Home Screen, or in a Notebook Section, the Options pane will only have three options, Sync, Sync Error, and Settings. However, if you are in a section editing pages, then the Options pane will also have a Create New Page button. Should you be viewing a note, then the Create New Page button will become a Delete Page button instead.

The purpose of the different buttons is as follows:

- **Delete page:** Deletes the page you are viewing

- **New Page:** Creates a new page in the section that you are viewing

- **Settings:** Most of the settings that you can change in One Note for Android can be found when you click this button

- **Sync:** Clicking this button will sync the current page with the notebook saved on your One Drive cloud storage space

- **Sync Error:** This only lights up when there has been an error syncing the note with One Drive. Click on the icon when it appears to gather more information on the error

Once you open the Settings menu, you will be able to modify certain things about One Note For Android. Some of the options available to you in this menu include:

- **Sync on Wi-Fi only:** by tapping this checkbox, you will be confirming that you will only be able to sync notes and notebooks with One Drive when you are connected to Wi-Fi. This will help you to conserve your mobile data.

- **Windows Live ID Account:**should you ever want to view the account that you are logged in to while using One Drive for Android this is the button you should tap. Usually, you are redirected to a window in the Android settings app, not One Note itself. In the app, there is another options button in the upper right corner of the screen that you can press to either Sync Now, Remove Account or access Help. The Help feature opens a webpage in your browser that allows you to view the help documentation that is related to your device.

- **Upgrade:** One Note for Android is usually free for the first 500 notes, after which you will not be able to edit or create any more notes until you delete some. However, if you pay a small fee, you can upgrade your One Note for Android app so that you can edit unlimited notes

- **Help:** Clicking on help opens a webpage in your default web browser that contains all the help information for your particular device.

- **Support:** Tapping on support will bring up your web browser, and load the different support forums that have been started on the Microsoft website for One Note for Android

- **Use Terms:** Tapping this will bring up a pop-up window that will display the apps terms of use

- **Privacy Statement:** Tapping on this will bring up a tab in your default web browser that will display Microsoft's privacy statement.

- **Third Party Notice:** This item will bring up a pop up window that will give you more information about any third-party technologies that you are using in Microsoft One Note for Android

- **Version:** Tapping this will give you more information on the version of One Note for Android that you are using

- **Copyright:** Tapping this option will display the copyright language for the app.

Despite the fact that it is a prominent feature in both One Note for iOS and Desktop versions of One Note, you cannot change the settings for picture quality on One Note for Android. This means that some of your photos may appear to have a lower quality than they actually do, while others will be viewed in their full scale, regardless of what you try.

There are some One Note settings that are not available from within the app itself, but are available through the device settings. To view those settings, you will have to tap the settings icon on your device and select the One Note app in the list of installed apps. Some of the options that are not available via the app but are available in your device's app menu include:

- **Force Stop:** Tapping this button allows you to stop One Note and close it if it will not close any other way. It stops all processes pertaining to the program.

- **Uninstall:** Tapping this button will uninstall the app from your device

- **Clear Data:** Tapping on this button will temporarily clear all the data that is stored on your device by the application. However, when you log in again, the data that had been cleared will be restored.

- **Clear Cache:** This button will clear all the information that One Note has stored on your system Cache. If the app is misbehaving, you can try to tap this button after you have tapped on Force Stop, then restart the app.

Chapter 9:

One Note for iOS Devices

As the first non-windows devices to receive One Note, the iPad, iPod touch and iPhone were given greater focus, and for that reason, the interfaces on these devices is much better than that on the Android version of the application. In fact, One Note for iOS is even more advanced than One Note for Windows Phone, though it still has fewer functions than One Note for Windows and even the One Note web application.

The One Note for iOS Interface

Navigating through One Note for iOS is a unique experience, as many of the cool features, animations and styles that are used have been optimized to run on Apple devices. All iOS devices, except the iPad have basically the same interface, and the only real difference between the interface on the iPad and other iOS devices is the size of the display, which makes the interface look dramatically different on the iPad.

There are two different orientations used in One Note for iPad, Landscape and Portrait. In Landscape view, you have access to a navigation bar on the left side of the screen, and the note pane is on the right. However, in portrait mode, the navigation pane disappears, and all you have is the note pane that fills the whole screen. The navigation bar is accessed via an icon on the left side of the screen.

On the iPhone and iPod Touch, each pane takes up the whole display, and the buttons are all placed at the top and bottom of the screen. Some of the main features of the interface on the One Note for iOS devices include:

- **The Note Pane:** The note pane usually takes up the whole display when in portrait, and two thirds of the screen in Landscape orientation in the iPad version. It looks like a piece of paper in a ring binder on the iPad. For the other iOS devices, the pane takes up the whole display, much like it does on the iPad in portrait orientation, just smaller. Above the note pane you can see where you are in the notebook.To change locations in the notebook or section that you are viewing, all you have to do is tap on the name of the notebook or section that you would like to view and you will be redirected straight to that section or notebook. For instance, if you would like to view a list of pages that are in a particular section, all you have to do is tap on the name of the section. If you would like to view a list of the sections in the notebook, tap on the notebook name and a list of all the sections in the notebook shall be displayed.

- **The List Pane:** This pane is where you can view a list of your notebooks, the sections contained in a notebook, and the pages that are in a section. To view an item, all you have to do is tap it and it will be displayed below all pinned items. The Recents tab creates a pin icon on the right of every item you have viewed. By tapping this icon, you can move the item to the top of the list regardless of the item that you have touched. The item that you pin next will go below the top item and so on.

- **The Back Button:** The back button appears in the upper left corner of the display on every window except the home page. The button resembles a left facing arrow, and tapping it will take you to any section, note or list that you were viewing previously. Depending on where the button will take you and where you are in the notebook, the text that accompanies the back button will change. For instance, if you are viewing notebook sections, the button will display home, however, if you are displaying a particular page in a section of a notebook, it will display the name of the notebook. It is important to remember that regardless of the text that the button displays, its primary function is a back button.

- **New Section Button:** This button appears next to the back button everywhere except on the home screen

- **View Icons/Search Button:** The bottom of the window contains three buttons that you can tap to change what you view on the display. The first changes the view of the list pane and shows you any unfiled notes that you may have, the next button displays recent notes, and the third brings up the search view.

- **Keyboard:** once you have opened a note, when you click on the pane a keyboard will appear automatically. The keyboard on iOS devices has its own functions including a check box button that you can tap to add check boxes to items that you have selected, and a bullet button that adds bullets to the selected text. It also contains a camera button that allows you to take photos to add to a note, or to add pictures to the note, and a return button that changes depending on where you are in the app. For instance, if you are trying to log in, the button will display Sign In, while if you are trying to search for something, the button will read Search rather than Return. If you would like to close the keyboard, just tap on the close keyboard button on the bottom right on of the keyboard.

Creating and Editing Notes in One Note for iOS

When it comes to creating, writing and editing notes on One Note for iOS, the process has been made as simple as possible, though you must remember that the app has fewer features than its online and desktop counterparts.

Creating a new note is simple and can be done regardless of where you are in the application. All you have to do is tap the new note icon in the upper right hand corner of the window to reveal a pop up menu with two options, Create Note (Unfiled) or Create Note in Current Section. The first choice creates a new note in your Web or Personal notebook and stores it under Unfiled Notes, while the second option creates a note in whatever section displayed at the top of the window, regardless of where you are in the application. If you are actually viewing the Web notebook's unfiled section and you click on the New Note option then the second option will be unavailable because it is basically redundant.

If you would like to open an existing note from Microsoft One Drive that is relatively simple as well. All you have to do is access the home screen and tap the name of the notebook, the name of the section, and the name of the note that you wish to access.

Adding a picture is also very simple, and can be done by tapping on the camera icon at the top of the keyboard. You will then be presented with two options:

1. **Camera:** Tapping on camera will activate your iOS device's camera, allowing you to take a picture that you can then add to your note. The camera interface is relatively easy to understand, and even has a button that can change the camera you are using between the rear camera and the front camera. After you take your picture, two icons will appear at the bottom of the screen, the one of the left allows you to discard the photo you just took and take a new one, while the one on the right confirms that the photo you have been taken is the one that you would like to insert into the app.

2. **Photo Library:** Tapping on this option will allow you to choose an item from your device's photo library

If your device does not have a camera, then you will be presented with two different options, Saved Pictures and Photo Stream.

When it comes to renaming notes and notebooks, the procedure is much the same as with the One Note for Android App, with many of the same restrictions. This means that you can edit the name of a note, but you cannot edit the name of a section or the whole notebook without logging on to the One Note web app or desktop application. You also cannot create a new notebook in One Note for iOS.

However, you can delete notes in the iOS app using one of two procedures

1. Swipe the note item to the left in the list pane. A red delete button will appear, and if you are sure that you would like to delete the note then you can tap delete and the note will disappear.

2. Tapping the trash can icon at the top of the display will bring up a menu with an option to delete a page, if you are sure you want to delete the page tap the Delete This Page option and the note will disappear.

Searching through Notes in One Note for iOS

Searching through notes in One Note for iOS is much the same as searching through notes on the web and desktop applications, and the search feature allows you to search for single terms in the notes contained in all the different notebooks. However, due to the limited functionality of the app compared to the desktop version, you can only search for text within notes, and you cannot search for pictures or tags.

Searching for text in One Note for iOS is as simple as tapping the search button at the bottom of the screen and type the search term into the Search Notebooks field at the top of the list pane. The results of your search should appear in the list pane below the search field. Once you have found the note that you would like to edit, you can view it in the note pane by tapping it. You will not lose any of your search results when you do this as the list pane will not be affected by your tapping on the note.

Managing notebooks on One Note for iOS app has been made extremely difficult, and the only way to effectively rename, delete or move notebooks is through the One Drive app for iOS.

Configuring One Note for iOS

One Note for iOS has very few settings that you can actually modify. To change the settings that are available to you in the app, the first thing you must do is tap the settings button at the top of the home screen. The window that opens has a number of options including:

1. **Upgrade:** Like One Note for Android, One Note for iOS limits the number of notes that you can have to 500. However, you can have unlimited notes if you pay a nominal fee to upgrade the app.

2. **Sync Now:** Tapping on this item immediately syncs all notes that are programmed to sync automatically

3. **Notebook Settings:** This button allows you to choose which notebooks to sync automatically while simultaneously allowing you to choose which notebooks will be displayed on the home screen

4. **Image Size:** A feature that is notably absent from its Android counterpart, the image size setting allows you to select the size of the images that you insert into different notes

5. **Sign Out:** Tapping this button will sign you out of One Note

6. **Help and Support:** Tapping this button will open a window that gives you links to different community support forums and help documentation

7. **Terms of Service:** Tap this button if you would like to view One Note's terms of service

8. **Privacy:** Tap this button if you would like to view One Note's privacy settings

Just like with its Android counterpart, One Note for iOS has some settings that you cannot change within the app, but that you can change using your device's settings. To access these settings, tap on the settings icon on your device, and tap on the One Note icon in the settings pane. The settings that appear are outlined below:

1. **Sync on Wi-Fi Only:** This particular option ensures that notebooks will only sync with One Drive when you are within Wi-Fi range. This allows you to keep the data usage of the app to a minimum, and ensures that you do not go over your data limit.

2. **Reset Application**: This feature is especially useful when you have sync errors, or other errors that will not fix themselves regardless of how many times you restart the application. Once activated, you will have to sign yourself back in to One Note, but you will not lose any information

3. **Version**: There is nothing you can do to change this setting as it is just a description of the version of the app that you currently have installed on your device.

Managing Syncing and Images in One Note for iOS

Setting individual notes to sync automatically is something that may seem unnecessary, but is one of the most useful features of One Note for iOS, especially if they are set up so that they sync regardless of whether you can see them on the home screen or not. The steps below outline how to turn OFF automatic syncing for particular notebooks, though following the opposite of this procedure will turn ON syncing for any notes that you may have created:

1. When you are viewing the home screen, tap the settings button at the top of the screen and tap on notebook settings. A pop up window should appear

2. Tap on the on slider that is next to a notebook to turn syncing off for that particular note. Once the slider is in the off position, you will not be able to view the notebook on the homepage, and the note will not sync automatically.

3. Close the settings pane by tapping on the settings button and then tapping the close button in the upper right hand corner of the window. Once you return to the Home screen, you will realize that the notes that you have toggled off are no longer visible, and they will not sync automatically.

Managing image settings on One Note for iOS is simple despite the fact that there are quite a few options to choose from when it comes to how you would like the app to display photos. For instance, you can choose from a wide range of image sizes when you are inserting the images to notes:

- Small sets the images to .5 megapixels

- Medium sets the images to 1 megapixel

- Large sets the images to 2 megapixels

- Actual Size will display the photo in notes at their actual sizes

- Ask me will ensure that you receive a prompt every time you try to insert an image in a note so that you can determine for yourself how large the image should be when it is being inserted into the note.

Chapter 10: Top 10 Tips for One Note Users

There are many tips and tricks that have been outlined in this book that will make using One Note that much simpler. There are also many scenarios that have been described that show you how useful the application can be. This chapter aims to emphasize some of these points, while simultaneously give you a few tips which could make your use of the program easier.

1. Backing up Important Data

Syncing and backing up of notes and notebooks has been discussed at length in various sections of this book, but the importance of this feature needs to be emphasized one more time so that you can truly understand how useful the feature can be.

Consider this scenario, you are on your way to Europe from the West coast for a well-deserved vacation and need to catch a connecting flight in New York. However, when you arrive in New York, you realize that you have lost your hand luggage, and that it had all the information you need for your trip.

However, you still have your cell phone, and you remember that your itinerary was saved in One Note, which you can access through your phone. Because of the data backup, you make it to your next plane with barely a moment to spare, but you find it, and you're on your way to Barcelona.

Another scenario where you could be saved by the backup feature on one note this, you are on your way for a job interview, but you forget to bring and review your resume to the meeting. However, you have backed everything up on One Note and you have your iPad with you. You go for the interview anyway, and when you are asked for your resume, you hand over your iPad with all the information that your future employer needs on it. You never know, you may ace the interview purely because you have your resume on an iPad.

Perhaps you were on your way for a meeting at work and you forgot to carry that report that was due today because you were more occupied with chowing down breakfast and getting out of the house as fast as you can. Now you are two hours away from home and the meeting is in an hour. Then you remember that you have the presentation on One Note and all you have to do is print out the hard copies and connect your phone to the projector and you're sorted.

The number of scenarios that One Note could help with are limitless, but the examples outlined above should be enough to show just how important the application can be.

2. You Have Access To Entire Office Documents On Your Phone At The Touch Of A Button

One Note is one of the only office apps that allows you to access documents easily on Android. Despite the fact that you may not be able to work much on your documents, you will at least be able to access and view them on your mobile device.

This feature is especially useful when you realize that saving the document as a printout on One Note rather than pasting it in to the application will allow you to view it exactly the same way you would in the original program. You may not be able to edit the documents, but you will at least be able to view them perfectly in One Note. If you have the One Drive application on your phone, you can access Word, Excel and PowerPoint documents via the appropriate web applications and actually edit the files, though you will have limited features compared to the full office applications.

3. Dictating Notes to Text

This is another feature that has been addressed in earlier chapters, but its importance cannot be emphasized. Though this feature is most useful in One Note for Android as it does not allow you to store recorded voice notes, it is a very useful option that should be seen as an added feature rather than a missing option, especially if that was your aim in the first place. This feature is especially useful for those people that have to translate a lot of dictated audio into plain text.

4. Retrieving Text from Images

This feature has been discussed at length in previous chapters, but its importance cannot be overstated, especially for those people who work with images on a regular basis. The fact that it is so easy to do is one of the best things about this feature, however, it is important to note that you have to ensure that your photograph is of the highest quality possible to ensure that the text that you are trying to grab from the image comes out as clearly as possible.

You must also ensure that the photo is not too dark or too bright, and that the font in the picture is not one of those difficult to read calligraphic fonts that are sometimes used, especially by creative individuals. However, in most cases, even if the picture is dark or the font is hard to read, you will still be able to retrieve at least some of the text, meaning you will be able to avoid most of the retyping that you need to do.

5. Taking a Screengrab and Marking it

As was mentioned previously, one of the best things about One Note is that you can take a screen shot of something using the clipping tool in the application. You can then use the pen tool in One Note to mark up the image. This is a very useful feature especially if you would like to add notes and comments to a photograph or image and share it for the world to see. For instance, if you are in the middle of developing a website and you would like to show your contributors what you would like to keep or change in the website, you can use the pen tool to note anything that you feel should be noted.

If you do not have a computer to a PC that has digital pen technology, you could always use actual text, or you could even use your mouse pointer as a pen and draw your comments if your handwriting with the mouse is good enough.

6. Marking Up Documents with a Pen

Should you be able to access a digital pen-capable PC, you will realize that marking up documents in One Note is easy. However, if you would like to ensure that you keep some of the similarities to the original document's formatting, then you will find it is easier to import a printout of the document instead of copy/pasting the contents of a page or document onto the note page.

If you have access to other Microsoft Office applications on your pen-capable PC then there are some cases where you could use the pen to mark up the documents in that app in much the same way. However, you must keep in mind that it can be trickier to do so in those apps, so it may be easier to just stick to One Note when marking up documents.

7. Copying links into Paragraphs

If you ever need to create links to specific parts of a One Note page, you can do it easily by right-clicking on the paragraph or note container that you would like to link and clicking on the Copy Link to Paragraph option. This will allow you to copy a link to your computer's clipboard, and you can then add that link to any document of your choice.

8. Searching Text In Images

This is another feature that has been addressed before but cannot be emphasized enough. The ability to search for text in images means that any image that you drop into One Note that has text in it can be discovered as long as you make the text in the image searchable. Even better, you can specify the language that the text is in so that you can find it later. This will allow you to find images quickly regardless of the language that the text in the photograph is in.

9. Docking One Note to the Desktop

If you find yourself using One Note regularly, you can make sure that it is always within easy reach by placing it beneath all your other open windows. This will ensure that you do not always have to select it from the taskbar, and that you can edit your notebooks whenever you need to without much hassle.

To dock One Note to your desktop, all you have to do is click on the view tab and click on the Dock to Desktop option and the app will automatically dock itself to the desktop below all the other open windows. Other windows may move a little, but you will always be able to see all the information displayed in them, as well as the information displayed in One Note. However, it must be noted that this feature works best if you have a large monitor screen as resizing the windows may make text hard to read.

10. Creating Outlook Tasks in One Note

One of the most useful features of One Note is the ability to create Outlook tasks that can then be modified at a later date. These tasks are created and edited via a drop-down menu in One Note. The menu has a range of options that include options to delete or open a task in Microsoft Outlook. The tasks that you create will add themselves to your Outlook automatically as long as you have set up and configured the application on the same computer that you are using One Note on.

It is important to remember that you do not have to create a new task then add the task information to it. It is much simpler to choose an existing item and then select an option from the drop-down menu that is displayed on the screen. Once you have selected the appropriate option, the item will immediately be made a task.

Conclusion

OneNote is one of the most versatile note taking applications on the planet, and is well suited for a wide variety of people from doctors and lawyers to students and researchers, to those people who just love to write things everywhere so that they will not forget them.

If you are one of those people who has never experienced a program or application like this then be warned, this program is addictive. The countless features and endless possibilities will keep you staring at the screen for hours, regardless of whether you are using your smartphone, laptop or PC.

The way it integrates seamlessly with the other programs in the Microsoft Office Suite is also very impressive and is something that you will soon be taking for granted once you get comfortable using the program.

Though OneNote is defined as a free-form information gathering computer program, it is way more than that. It is an organizer, a spreadsheet application, a database management system, a word processor, and countless other things rolled into one.

Although it is not geared towards publishing work, because it integrates so well with the rest of Microsoft Office you do not really need to worry about that. What you do need to pay attention to is the fact that it will make doing your work much

Conclusion

easier, and when you feel you have done enough to publish it, you can just transfer it to one of the other programs in the Office Suite to polish it off before releasing it to the world.

This manual has given you a peek into the world that is OneNote. It is a world that is ever changing and full of possibility, and if you choose to enter it, you will never be disappointed.